EDUCATION DENIED

EDUCATION DENIED

CHILDREN CHALLENGES CHOICES

Bernard Gassaway

Published by Gassaway ALG, Hempstead, New York

Copyright © Copyright © 2016, 2018 by Bernard Gassaway

ISBN: 978-0-9769709-3-4

Library of Congress Control Number: 2015919290

All rights reserved.

No part of this publication may be reproduced or transmitted in any form or by any means, electronic or mechanical, including photocopy, recording, or any information storage and retrieval system, without permission in writing from the publisher.

Printed in the United States of America
Website: www.bernardgassaway.com
Twitter: @DrGassaway
Email: bgassaway1@gmail.com

Designed by Vince Pannullo

Contents

Dedication 7
Note to Readers 9
Acknowledgments 13
About the Author 15
Preface 17
Introduction: Education Denied 19

Book I:
    Children 23
    A Teacher's Sin: Learn the Language of Pain 25
    Mother Nature: Observe and Learn 29
    Colored Boys: Colorful Behavior 31
    School Trip to Court: An Ounce of Prevention 33
    Relationships: Fifteen Ways to Build Relationships
        with Children 35
    Action Plan for Children: *Invisible Black Boys become*
        Invisible Black Men Unless… 39

Book II:
    Challenges 49
    Segregation: Unequal Schools 51
    The Parent Factor: Parents as Predictor of a Child's
        Success in Schools 53
    School System Sanctioned Cheating: Credit Recovery 57
    Politicians or Pimps: Does it Make a Difference for School
        Children? 61
    School-to-Prison Pipeline: A By-product of Educational
        Inequity 65

A Parent's Cry for Help: A Case for Collaboration,
    not Condemnation 69
Action Plan for Parents: *Parents, Mind Your Own Business* 73

Book III:
    Choices... 81
    Leadership in Practice: Decision-making................................ 83
    Prison-to-School Pipeline: Reversal of Misfortunes............... 89
    Million Dollar Teachers: It's Time for Change 93
    Fathers: Unwelcomed in Urban Schools................................. 97
    Action Plan for Community: *An Open Letter to Black Clergy*............. 101

Book IV:
    Reflections 107
    Pupil of the Year: A Personal Reflection - 1977 109
    Mentor Me.. 113
    Leadership: A Look Back... 115
    Do Fathers Matter: My Father.. 119
    Action Plan for School Personnel: *School Revolution,*
        not Reform 121

Book V:
    Compilation of Published Articles 127
    Teachers 127
    Blame Game: A Game Without Winners............................. 131
    Suicide by Educator.. 133
    The New York City School System Is Not Broken 139
    Unprotected Children... 143
    Action Plan for Policymakers: *The Mis-Evaluation of*
        Governor Andrew Cuomo... 147

References 151

Dedication

ATIYA, you are the daughter that brings light into my darkness. You inspire your peers to dream, to hope and to act. You remind adults of the freedom they yearned for as children, and now, still, as your name implies, you are A Gift from God.

I love you infinitely!

Without education, you are not going anywhere in this world.
—*Malcolm X*

Note to Readers

I thank you for reading my work. I believe we are inspired by different things at different times. My words are written to provide clues for those like me who are seeking answers. I believe the day we stop questioning is the day we stop living.

CELEBRATE CHILDREN

Acknowledgments

I appreciate all of my past, present and future students who have and who will continue to inspire me.

My daughter Atiya, the light of my life, continues to inspire me to dream and hope for a better future for our children and their children.

I appreciate and thank all of my teachers, especially those who believed in me when I did not believe in myself.

I thank Annie Gassaway for the greatest gift: My life. She continues to be my most significant and beloved Angel. I feel her love and protection every single day.

I thank God for the hourly and daily miracles.

Change requires courage.

—Bernard Gassaway

About the Author

BERNARD Gassaway is a student and a teacher. As a student, he strives to discover how to become the ultimate learner. As a teacher, he strives to enable and empower his students to discover their life's passions through inquiry and deliberation.

Bernard has served as a teacher, assistant principal, principal, superintendent and community stakeholder in New York City. In each capacity, he has relied on his childhood experiences to serve as an anchor for his guiding principles and theory of action.

Bernard earned his B.A. in English from Le Moyne College, Syracuse, N.Y., M.P.A. from SUNY at Albany, Albany, N.Y., Master's of Education and Supervision from Baruch College, N.Y., N.Y., Master's of Education from Columbia University's Teachers College, N.Y. and Doctor of Education from Columbia University's Teachers College.

Of all of Bernard's accomplishments, he is most proud of his role as father to Atiya Lilly-Gassaway. She continues to help shape him as a leading national educational leader and teacher.

Bernard was born in Macon, Georgia but raised in Brooklyn, New York along with his six siblings. He currently resides in Hempstead, New York.

Preface

THIS book provides thought-provoking anecdotes that are meant to motivate the reader to act. Passive participation serves to maintain the status quo.

Over the last nine years, from 2006 to 2015, I have written numerous articles—some for publication, and others for this specific book. The contents of this book consist of a combination of some of my published and unpublished works.

These works capture the essence of what I have experienced as an urban school educator. I hope the reader will be able to learn from my experiences. I also hope that the reader will be motivated to take action, in his or her own way, on behalf of children and families.

I wrote this book to highlight challenges that children, families, communities, stakeholders and school personnel (particularly in urban centers) face when attempting to educate children. I believe urban school children are denied a quality education for a host of reasons, some which are explicitly and implicitly stated throughout this text (Schott Foundation, 2015).

I use several approaches to inform, motivate and inspire the reader to do whatever is within his or her purview to improve the quality of education for children. I tell stories. I share anecdotes. I give specific instructions. I make recommendations.

The book is organized into five sections. Each section ends with an action plan. These plans are articles that I published previously but are directly germane to what is shared in the section where they appear. Each action plan provides specific instructions or recommendations for parents, teachers, administrators, community stakeholders or policymakers.

I hope for each reader to pause and reflect after reading each section. The power of reflection can be transformative.

Education is the most powerful weapon which you can use to change the world.

—*Nelson Mandela*

INTRODUCTION: EDUCATION DENIED

EDUCATION is denied to millions of urban poor children because urban educators, politicians and policymakers lack the courage to correct the course of failed policies and practices that are rooted in racial, socioeconomic and political inequities (Rothstein, 2014).

Schools in poor urban centers are expected to educate children who are faced with enormous challenges. For example, many poor urban district and school personnel are expected to successfully educate children who are often homeless, pregnant, formerly incarcerated, in foster care, have limited English proficiency, have special needs, live in single-family households, are juvenile delinquents, illiterate and/or poor. School leaders and teachers are expected to demonstrate success by raising test scores and graduation rates. They are expected to do this with limited resources (Lacour & Tissington, 2011; Payne, 2008; Sharkey, 2010).

Because our urban educators, policymakers and politicians lack the courage to address racial, socioeconomic and political inequities, they propagate a false premise of achievement among the poor. Listen to them boast about progress when reading and math proficiency rates increase by a few percentage points (Brody, 2014). They do not focus on the fact that the majority of poor children are not proficient. Others boast about increases in graduation rates, without mentioning that college readiness rates are decreasing. How do you celebrate more students graduating but fail to acknowledge they are not being prepared for the next level (Glancy et al., 2014)?

Education will continue to be denied to poor children as long as social, racial, economic and political realities are ignored. Just as a divided house cannot stand, a divided education system cannot work for all children. Poor children do not receive the same quality of education that rich or wealthier children receive (OECD, 2013; Rothstein & Santow, 2012).

When we examine what makes schools in wealthy communities work, we find families that value education, children who are ready to learn, an abundance of resources (e.g., family income and community wealth), communities that value education and highly effective teachers. Because these factors are not as evident in poor urban communities, the achievement levels between the rich and the poor widen, thus the achievement gap widens as well (Ferguson et al., 2007; Reardon, 2011; Schott Foundation, 2015).

Failure to acknowledge an achievement gap is senseless. Of course there is an achievement gap. There is a resource gap. There is an opportunity gap. There is a value gap. There is a family gap. There is a community gap. When you combine these gaps, you have an educational chasm (Ferguson et al., 2007; Reardon, 2011; Schott Foundation, 2015).

What follows are some stories, anecdotes, suggestions and recommendations that may provide reasons to motivate educators, parents, policymakers, politicians and community stakeholders to take courageously sound actions to correct the course of educational inequities and harmful social policies that perpetuate conditions that continue to deny poor children quality learning opportunuties.

Book I

Educating the mind without educating the heart is no education at all.

—*Aristotle*

Children

BE quiet. Shut up. Stop talking. Be silent. Say nothing. Keep quiet. Silence is golden. Why are you talking? You never stop talking. You talk too much.

"Good morning boys and girls. My name is Ms. School. I am your teacher. Before we go any further, I need to teach you two things. Your first lesson is to learn how to be quiet. When I hold up two fingers, that means you must be quiet. Your second lesson is to be quiet when I am speaking. Never interrupt me when I am talking. If you follow these two simple rules, everything will be all right. Okay? I don't hear you. Very good!"

A child without education is like a bird without wings.

—*Tibetan proverb*

A Teacher's Sin: Learn the Language of Pain

WHEN you think about your primary- and secondary-school experiences, it is the teacher who brings a smile or frown to your face. Often, one has fond memories of at least one teacher. That teacher may have had a profound effect on your life's direction. Teachers either feed or extinguish dreams. Arguably, next to parents, teachers are the most significant adults in the lives of children.

Not quite two months into my teaching career, I learned my most valuable lesson: what it meant to be an adult among children. No college course could have prepared me for the letter I received from one of my students. The letter, dated December 11, 1986, described the horrific living conditions of this student.

In many ways, I experienced the typical urban school when I began as a teacher. On October 14, 1986, I was given a sixth-grade class that had three teachers prior to my arrival. I strongly believed, and it might have been expressed by the students, that they were intent on running me out of the class, as they had successfully done with the previous teachers. In short, they gave me hell. They talked nonstop. They yelled. I yelled. I was exhausted after the constant chaos, challenges and confusion. The students were about to achieve their goal. I was going to quit. I asked the principal for help on how to handle the students' behavior. He basically said close the door and do what you have to do. I took that to mean drop the script that I had written for myself. I was not good at acting like a teacher. I needed to be Bernard. Up to that point, I was not prepared to deal with students who were in pain. I thought I would prepare a lesson and teach it. I had no idea that students had issues, barriers and concerns that would preclude me from teaching them. My daily agenda did not consider their painful realities. They used the weapons that they had: profanity and insults.

As a 26-year-old teacher without any official training for my new role, I thought it was appropriate to exchange insults with students. I was more street than school. If they called me a name, I would respond in kind.

One particular student, the one who wrote the letter, found some reason to insult me daily. I found this odd because other students said mean and insulting things to her daily. No one wanted to sit near her because of her body odor. She would not lash out at them, only at me. At the time, I did not understand why.

On a day early in December 1986, I made an insulting remark that hit home for this student. Later that week, I received a letter from her. In her letter, she apologized for insulting me and for her behavior. She went on to explain why she came to school the way she did. She described her third-world existence. I cried after reading the letter. I also made arrangements with my mother-in-law, who was a beautician, to do her hair. This was my attempt to seek repentance.

From this experience, I learned many valuable lessons. Children express pain in so many ways. As a teacher, I needed to learn the language of pain. While I experienced my own pain as a child, as an adult I was unable, at that time, to understand the pain of my students. This was ironic because when I was a student, like my students, I expressed myself through pain. I verbally and physically lashed out at teachers. So, I was familiar with the language of pain.

I addressed the language of pain by focusing on the needs of my students, needs that went beyond reading, writing and arithmetic. I learned that my students' insults about my mother and me were a reflection of their reluctance to establish a relationship with me for fear of abandonment. I surmised that they had experienced abandonment at home and at school. I could count on one hand how many of my students had fathers in their lives.

It was only after I learned to reflect on my own childhood, which was not unlike my students', that I understood the language of pain. This helped me to establish meaningful relationships with my students. I convinced them that

I was not leaving, as those three teachers had before I arrived on that October day in 1986. We then began to shift from insults to instruction.

The roots of education are bitter, but the fruit is sweet.

—*Aristotle*

Mother Nature: Observe and Learn

On one occasion, while watching a show about horses on public access television, I observed a horse in its natural habitat nudging its newborn foal, which was lying on the grass, apparently unable to stand. Without warning, the mother unleashed what appeared to be blind fury, clinching the foal by the neck with her jaws and violently flailing it about. Other horses quickly approached her [as if to stop her], but they were too late. Within seconds, the foal was dead. I surmised that the mother had decided to kill her newborn rather than see it die a slow death.

As I reflect on my observations of nature, I am reminded of the numerous times when I have been perplexed by how we treat our children. When I see six-year-old children trying to navigate four-lane street crossings, I ask, "Who cares about these children?" When I see first-grade children carrying heavy knapsacks, walking to school alone, I ask, "Who cares about these children?" When I see children hanging out on the streets after 10 P.M. on weeknights and weekends, I ask, "Who cares about these children?" When I see thousands of children between the ages of 12 and 18 incarcerated, I ask, "Who cares about these children?"

Children silently ask themselves similar questions. I believe that, in the absence of being appropriately nurtured and protected, children will ultimately adopt the rules of engagement set by their peers in order to survive.

Adults often characterize this behavior as peer pressure. I see it as an act borne out of a desire to survive. Notice how children, like other mammals, adapt to their environments in order to survive. They appear larger by puffing up and wearing extra large clothing when they only require a small or medium. They use camouflage effectively. While they do sometimes dress to impress, more often they dress to survive.

I have come to the conclusion that children are considered insignificant and dispensable by adults. They are expendable in the minds and hearts of many. How else can we explain the way we treat them around the world, in so-called "developed" and "underdeveloped" countries alike? In the United States of America, what is our excuse?

As I think about our children, I am reminded of what occurs annually on the African plains of Tanzania. Each year on the Serengeti, the wildebeests and zebras begin their great migration. To reach their destination, they must cross gulfs of water. There is one problem they must anticipate every year: alligators await their arrival. The alligators wait to devour the slow and the weak.

In some ways, the same is true of our educational system. Students who are slow and weak are devoured. They are consumed by greed. Children labeled as "special needs" are funded at higher rates than "regular" children. Poor children are likely to be tracked in a slow class, held back, given the weakest and least experienced teachers and forced to attend schools in the worst buildings and neighborhoods.

Just as the wildebeests and zebras must traverse the treacherous waters, our children must walk to school through neighborhoods that have little to no mercy for them. Countless assaults on children go unreported because it has become a community norm not to report alleged crimes—even when the perpetrators are known.

We have many lessons to learn from Mother Nature. My daughter and I visited zoos frequently when she was very young. As we observed animal behavior, I often found myself thinking, "Why can't we behave as animals?" Do we?

Colored Boys: Colorful Behavior

As I think about public education, federal legislation, school reform, differentiated instruction, multiple intelligences and parental involvement, I wonder what can be done to help the colored boys: Blue Boy, Green Boy, Gray Boy, Purple Boy and Black Boy. All of the traditional methods of instruction and discipline have not worked to improve their learning and behavior.

In school, Blue Boy walks the halls. Green Boy is frequently absent. Gray Boy fights all the time. Purple Boy sits in the back of the class and sleeps. Black Boy is very quiet but does no classwork. Blue Boy and Black Boy have been held back twice. They are 15. Green Boy, Gray Boy and Purple Boy have been held back once. They are 14. All of them are currently in the 8th grade. Physically, they stand tall and wide among their classmates. Black Boy even has facial hair.

The colored boys are restless in class. They frequently request, in their own way, a pass to leave the room: "Teacher, I got to go to the bathroom." Rather than argue with the colored boy, the teacher quickly signals him to take a pass. As the boy leaves the room, tension follows. The teacher quietly prays that the boy stays out for the remainder of the period. Some of his classmates pray the same prayer.

Frankly, the colored boys are not wanted in their school. They do not fit in. They are square pegs trying to fit into round holes. Teachers and administrators do not know how to deal with them. Staff can often be heard saying, "Those boys will probably end up dead or in jail." "They should be in special ed." "Where are their parents?"

Blue Boy currently lives in a foster home. Purple Boy lives with his great-grandmother. She is 53. Gray Boy lives with his mother and father. Green Boy lives with his mother. Black Boy lives with his father.

The colored boys cannot recall the last time they succeeded in school. Teachers' threats of failure fail to motivate them. For the colored boys, failure has become inconsequential, so they believe.

The colored boys are described by many as being handsome but with ugly ways. According to their teachers, "When you work with them one-on-one, they are sweet kids. When they get together, they are out of control! They cannot focus." They are famous and feared among their peers. The girls generally find them attractive; they stand out because of their colorful behavior.

Chinese fast food, boneless chicken and pork fried rice is their favorite meal. Before they come to school, they frequently stop at the corner bodega for breakfast: a 50-cent bag of potato chips, chocolate chip cookies, plain M&Ms and a grape soda. They refuse to eat school breakfast. That would not be cool. If they wanted school breakfast, they would have to come early. That too would not be cool.

As the colored boys get older, they are reclassified and placed in a larger cohort. Their names are replaced by numbers and labels such as at-risk, over-aged, truant, juvenile delinquent, dropout, criminal, convict, inmate, felon, mentally ill, homeless and unemployed. We exclude, isolate and incarcerate them until they disappear.

I wonder what can be done to help the colored boys before they become colored men.

School Trip to Court: An Ounce of Prevention

On a rainy June morning, along with a teacher and a member of a local community-based organization, I took ten middle school students to the New York City Queens County district attorney's office. It was certainly a day I will never forget. According to school officials, these students were the ones who frequently disrupted instruction or fought with each other. While waiting in front of the school to get copies of their permission slips, the principal came out to warn me about each student, describing past and predictable behaviors. I stopped her midway because I did not want to be influenced by her judgment and expectations.

We gathered the students and boarded a local public bus to the subway, and from there we made our way to the D.A.'s office on Queens Boulevard. After going through security screening, as was required of all visitors, we made our way to the special assistant to the district attorney. He welcomed us and was very generous with his time and that of his staff. He spoke to the students about the legal process and answered all of their questions. He even treated to them to lunch—pizza.

The students were taken on a tour of the facilities. One of the things that I am sure will remain in the students' minds and my own was the central booking process unit. This is where people are brought after arrest in order to be processed before being arraigned by a judge. This is where they are either released or transferred to the local jail until trial or until they make bail or go on trial.

The accused were separated by age into two groups, one for those ages sixteen and seventeen and another for those eighteen and older. I noticed that the younger detainees behaved differently than the older ones. They were loud and attempted to say things to the students as we walked by. The police officer said, "The loud ones are usually the punks. They are afraid, so they pretend to be tough." I said to myself, "This is similar to students who act out in class." Sure, some misbehave because they are bored. I would say a higher number act out because they are attempting to deflect classmates and teachers from their academic weaknesses. This is classic.

Another interesting moment was when the students were allowed to sit-in on a murder trial. The murder occurred in the students' community. Though they did not recognize the accused when he was identified by the judge, they were aware of the location of the murder. The judge, an African-American, was very nice. He stopped the proceedings to explain to the students what they were witnessing. The students were told prior to going into the courtroom that they must be extremely quiet. This worked for a short while. The students were gripped and sitting on the edge of their seats when the medical examiner testified. She explained how the bullet entered the deceased's abdomen and exited out by his groin area. Fascinating!

After about ten minutes in the courtroom, two of the boys began to make weird sounds and movements in their seats. After a few, "Shh, please be quiet and sit still" requests, I realized that these two students were not capable of sitting still for prolonged periods of time. In fact, I felt guilty—I set them up for failure. I am not a medical doctor or psychologist, but they probably had been diagnosed with ADHD or were simply hyperactive. Watching them attempt to sit still and stay quiet for a prolonged period of time was painful. We immediately left the courtroom, to the delight of all. I imagined the accused said to himself, "Get them the hell out of here!"

When we debriefed with our host, one student said, "I will never do anything to go to jail." Though our objective for the trip was not to "scare students straight," this experience served, at least for this one student, to show him a path he did not want to take in life.

Relationships: Fifteen Ways to Build Relationships with Children

1. *Create child-centered environments.* As you plan events, include children in the decision-making process. Encourage and respect their input. Unlike our current system of government where children have absolutely no voice—the voice of our children is the lifeblood of healthy learning environments.
2. *Learn how to listen to children.* Adults often reject a child's expressed logic and replace it with their own. "You do not really mean what you just said. You mean…" Do not offer a rapid-fire response once a child expresses himself. Let him see you think and consider his input.
3. *Create coordinated webs of support for children.* I often wonder why there is no visible network of city or not-for-profit agencies focusing on children. The current disjointed efforts minimize effectiveness. A coordinated, rather than a competitive, effort would yield greater results. City school systems function largely in isolation.
4. *Create experiences for children.* Rather than have them only read about the benefits of volunteerism, encourage them to volunteer at local hospitals, senior citizen homes or daycare centers. Children retain more of what they do than what they read. This leaves one to wonder, why do adults force children to spend so much time in artificial learning environments—schools?
5. *Demonstrate for children.* They will repeat more of what they see than what they hear. Adults talk too much. Speeches are overrated. "Talk is cheap!"

6. *Encourage children to play games.* Of all our childhood memories, we remember the games we used to play. "Miss Mary Mack, Mack, Mack, all dressed in black…" "Money on the wood makes the game go good." "Checkers, chess and monopoly." "Red light, green light, one, two, three." Ironically, fun and games have become antithetical to the perceived notion of a sound education. "You must get serious about life!" Why?
7. *Resist the pressure to transfer adult issues to children.* Allow children to enjoy their childhood before you begin to heap adult realities and responsibilities on them.
8. *Resist the temptation to tell children,* "I know how you feel." Instead say, "I think I understand how you feel based on what you said to me." You may even repeat what they said to you, to ensure clarity. This models active listening.
9. *Focus discussions with children in the present.* Adults tend to focus on the future—pensions, retirement or death. We also talk to children often about their future—college/career: "What do you want to be when you grow up?" Children focus more in the moment. Understanding where children are should help to improve communications between adults and them.
10. *Encourage children to come up with solutions to their problems.* Role-play is a good tool. Children love to act. They are natural performers.
11. *Take sense walks with children.* Walk around the neighborhood. Walk through the park. You can discuss what they see, hear, smell, feel and taste. Engage with them by disconnecting them from cell phones, social media or television.
12. *Make eye contact as you have discussions with them.* Again, listen more than you speak. It is more meaningful when children discover rather than when they are told, trained or conditioned.
13. *Play the question game with children.* Ask them five questions. Then have them ask you five questions. Complete several rounds of questions.
14. *Read to your children and have them read to you.* This is a very intimate

way to engage with children. Children sense that you care and are focused on them.

15. *Write letters to children.* Letter writing has become a lost art. Because computers exist, doesn't mean you need to use them as your only medium of communication. Use pen and paper and write notes to children. Have them write letters and notes to you as well.

Education is not preparation for life; education is life itself.

—John Dewey

ACTION PLAN FOR CHILDREN: INVISIBLE BLACK BOYS BECOME INVISIBLE BLACK MEN UNLESS...

> I am invisible, understand, simply because people refuse to see me.
> —Ralph Ellison

If we successfully educate Black boys in New York City, we kill the prison industry in New York State. If you want to know why young Black men are virtually invisible on college campuses throughout New York State, just visit juvenile detention centers and upstate prisons.

The Bloomberg and Klein administration must admit they have joined a line of administrations that failed to focus on the needs of the children who are most deprived by the New York City public school system. As with previous mayors and school chancellors, the Black male crisis has never been seen as a priority. This administration will not publicly acknowledge that there is a problem. More importantly, they have not offered a plan to address the problem that the system created and continues to perpetuate. To them, I ask, "What is your strategic or action plan to address the elephant in the room?" To them I say, "Black boys are routinely victimized by this school system." I contend, to paraphrase Ralph Ellison, "Black male students are invisible, understand, simply because the institutional racist school system refuses to see them."

As one example, let's look at what is happening with Black boys and special education. Black boys are being targeted for special education programs throughout this city. They are more susceptible to being classified with a handicapping condition because of the stereotypes that have been ascribed to them because of their race. They are considered angry, aggressive and dangerous. As a result, when Black boys show any level of independence or free will, school personnel routinely recommend them for special education placement. Black boys, who are developing normally, respond by outward aggression or total withdrawal when they feel unappreciated or disrespected by teachers.

Look at how my first and fifth-grade teachers described me nearly fifty years ago (Gassaway, 2006):

First grade: "Bernard is very aggressive at times. Sometimes refuses to answer you or do any work."

Fifth grade: "Bernard requires personal attention at times. He is a very fast worker, but he becomes restless at times. He seems to control his aggressiveness at this point."

As a child in the New York City school system, I was a victim of the aforementioned reality. I was not challenged intellectually. My reward for good work was to work independently with the SRA kit. When I became bored, I became restless. Then I got into trouble. The seeds were planted. Eventually, I was labeled and, yes, I became entangled in the juvenile "justice" system. I contend the same practices that led to my transgressions are happening to our Black boys today.

I have witnessed too many Black boys caught in the vortex of the educational/prison system.

To save our children, Black boys in particular, I propose that we begin to design and build schools that serve them. We need to start from pre-k. We need to design schools that support the physical development of young boys. This sit still, static approach to learning must be replaced by a dynamic learning environment. We must develop a living curriculum that is grounded in truth and relevance. School communities must be able to hire staff members who care about all children. This staff may be diverse in ethnicity but not in mission. We cannot allow incompetent, uncaring, diabolical teachers to destroy our Black boys.

What happens to our boys when they survive the school system?

Unfortunately, when our Black boys survive the public school system, we convince many of them to attend predominately-White colleges. We fail to warn them about the palpable racism they are likely to experience. What we do to them is shameful. It is another form of self-hatred. We convince them that true success can only be attained if they are in the presence of White people. As a result, many of these students fail to graduate unless they assimilate, thus, losing any sense of cultural identity.

Now, colleges across this country are struggling with what may be called the "Black male dilemma." Black male college students, the relatively few, are disappearing from campuses across this country. Even historically Black colleges are not immune. While on a recent college trip to Howard University, a student representative told a group of alternative school students that he was the only Black man in his calculus class, which had thirty students. This profound revelation underscores the harsh reality that we are losing many of our young Black men long before they reach adolescence. At this rate, schools like Morehouse may be forced to become coed in order to survive.

I have read about programs in higher education called the "Black Male Initiative." This initiative acknowledges that Black men are invisible on college campuses across this country. City University of New York established a committee to develop recommendations to address this reality. Their goal is to increase the presence and success of Black men in city colleges. To be successful with this initiative, one would need to figure out how to build a house without a foundation. While I applaud the intent of this initiative, I must say it may be an effort in futility as long as we live in a society where Black men are being destroyed during their childhood.

Are there any Black men in education policymaking positions?

The invisibility of Black men is not exclusive to the City University of New York. Let's look at Black male leadership within the New York City Department of Education. You can't find it. You will only see glimpses of it when the chancellor or mayor finds it convenient to put a few of them on parade to support a given initiative. Look over the mayor's left shoulder. That is where the Black, silent figure will be standing. You might as well place a mannequin to hold the spot.

The current leadership atrocity in the department of education (and likely citywide) reminds me of Douglas Turner Ward's play, *The Day of Absence*. In this satire, the town's people awoke to see that all Black people in the town had disappeared. White folks' homes were not cleaned; their clothes were not washed. Jails were emptied. This play was produced in 1965. Fast forward to the year 2006 [2015]. I began to think—Imagine if we had a 'day of absence' in the department of education (DOE)? Let's start with DOE headquarters. Other than the restrooms not being cleaned, and no security guards to scan visitors, business would run as usual. The majority of schools would be empty of students, except for specialized schools and schools in districts of choice and privilege. More than enough staff would be available to teach. You get my point.

You too can become invisible

I have learned that invisibility is not exclusive to Black people. If you are non-Black and work on behalf of Black children, you too become invisible. You may advocate for children but don't advocate too hard. You may be seen as "one of them." If you really put children first, watch your back. Your motives will be questioned. You will become a target. You see it is okay to create slogans such as "Children First." But don't you dare take it seriously, or else.

Principals and teachers are taught that if they want to truly advocate for children, find another line of work. Principals and teachers cannot teach children to have a voice if they themselves have been rendered voiceless. As a result, the victimization of children, Black boys, in particular, goes virtually unchallenged.

Recommendations

We must develop a multi-pronged approach:

1. Over the next five years, establish independent schools to serve approximately 100,000 children. Eventually increase this number to 200,000, which is roughly 20% of the public school enrollment. Focus on elementary and middle school students (Black boys particularly, not exclusively).
2. Change specific practices and policies in public education that are harming our children, particularly our Black boys (e.g., inappropriate special education classification).
3. Eliminate the wholesale, reprehensible practice of standardized testing. Start with elementary grades. This would free up millions of dollars for childcare. It will also increase instructional/learning time exponentially.
4. Develop teacher training centers in partnership with universities and colleges, public and private. This will also save millions of dollars for early childhood education.
5. Eliminate the Eurocentric curriculum in our public schools, particularly schools in non-European communities. Replace it with documents and other source material that address truth and relevance.
6. Demilitarize our schools. Replace school safety agents, vis-à-vis police personnel, with school community-based patrols. Hire senior citizens to provide school safety.
7. Combine elementary and secondary public schools with the college and university system. City University of New York Chancellor Matthew Goldstein may never publicly criticize public school's Chancellor Joel Klein because it would be politically incorrect. However, Chancellor Goldstein must admit that the public school system has failed to prepare students adequately for college. Therefore, I think the mayor should appoint one education commissioner to head all public education. This commissioner would be responsible for pre-k through university. Think of the possibilities.

If the mayor believes in the city's university system, he should give it the responsibility to train teachers. Think about it. With all of the schools of education within the city, both public and private, why does Chancellor Klein vis-à-vis the mayor spend millions of dollars per year to hire an Australian company to provide professional development for our teachers? Clearly, this is a vote of no confidence in the American college and university system.
8. Empower public school students to establish a union. This union must be free of adult involvement unless requested. This would provide students with a vehicle to exercise a free voice, free of toxic adult involvement.

Conclusion

To save our children, we must acknowledge that racism is the main reason why Black boys, in particular, in New York City, have never received a quality education. Therefore, we must begin to provide them with alternative learning communities that are free of racist ideologies and practices.

To save our children, we must eliminate racist policies and practices that perpetuate a cycle of poverty that breeds intra-community violence.

To save our children, we must save ourselves. Adults can no longer fantasize about the good ole days. Truth be told, those days never existed. We caught hell just like our children are catching hell.

To save our children, we must keep them in the nest a little while longer. We let go too soon. This is especially true of our boys. We expect too much of them, too soon.

To save our children, we must invest more in childcare than in prison-care. If we provide state of the art universal childcare for all children, the prison industry as we know it may become nearly obsolete. We must stop sacrificing our children, particularly our Black boys, to provide a livelihood for rural upstate communities, a place clearly where they depend on the prison industry for their economic survival.

Final Charge

Black men who have survived the system and have totally assimilated to the corporate model must come "home." To them I say, "Do not hate your children because they reflect the evils of our culturally deprived communities. Fulfill a moral and cultural obligation to use your talents and skills to change a life or two. Our Black boys are crying out for help. Instead of running away from them, we need to run toward them. Black boys cannot become successful and conscientious Black men without having successful and conscientious Black men in their lives.

Black men who have been assimilated to the criminal model, you too, must come "home." Our children need us now more than ever. We cannot brag about our criminal prowess. If you have children, get involved in their life. Once you demonstrate your true commitment to your children, they will innately forgive you for not being in their lives. I have seen too many children bewildered by the question of why. "Why isn't my father here?" I have silently asked myself that question a thousand times.

Education is the key to unlock the golden door of freedom.
—*George Washington Carver*

Book II

A child miseducated is a child lost.

—John F. Kennedy

Challenges

EACH year, principals must make a difficult decision. "Which children do I sacrifice this year?" Some children must be placed in the classrooms of the incompetent teachers.

Segregation: Unequal Schools

Was former Governor of Alabama George Wallace correct in 1963 when he declared in his inaugural speech, "segregation now, segregation tomorrow, segregation forever"? Today, millions across this country who live in segregated housing, attend segregated schools, and worship in segregated churches may respond "yes." Wallace's words seem prophetic, especially and ironically in northern cities such as New York, which was recently cited as having one of the most segregated school systems in America (Fessenden, 2012; Kucsera & Orfield, 2014).

It is worth looking back to a time not so long ago when states and local governments legally sanctioned segregation. Segregated schools, housing, and transportation, to mention a few, were protected by laws across the United States of America. In 1896, the U.S. Supreme Court ruled in *Plessy vs. Ferguson* that "separate but equal" was constitutional.

It was not until 1954, in the landmark decision in *Brown v. Board of Education of Topeka, Kansas*, that the "separate but equal" doctrine was overturned. The court unanimously ruled that "separate but equal was inherently unequal" and therefore unconstitutional.

Immediately following the *Brown* decision, it was believed laws and practices that had prohibited Black children from attending school with White children would be a thing of the past. It was further believed that equal access to quality education that was previously only afforded to White children would be equally afforded to Black children.

Fifty-one years after *Brown* and 52 years after Wallace's segregation declaration, there are segregated schools and communities abound across this country even though de jure segregation is now unconstitutional.

As I struggle to reject George Wallace's declaration of "segregation now, segregation tomorrow, segregation forever," I am forced to face the vestiges of past de jure segregation as well as the current conditions of de facto segregation. Regrettably, there are few if any signs to suggest that we may not face future de facto segregation—tomorrow and perhaps forever.

The American system of education, if unchanged, will continue to perpetuate its sad legacy of segregation and discrimination, most profoundly in elementary and secondary schools. As evidenced in all of the desegregation cases post-*Brown* 1954, segregated schools appear to be part of the fabric of American culture. There is no evidence based on the latest rounds of so-called school reforms, including Congress's Every Student Succeeds Act (2015), that segregation and unequal schools will be redressed.

The Parent Factor: Parents as Predictor of a Child's Success in Schools

"I love my mother and I know she loves me. She talks to me about school all the time. But school is not important to me. Truth be told, schoolwork has nothing to do with me. I know I need an education. School is not the only way to get it. I learn from my friends and watching TV. Anyway, there is a lot of drama in school. People do not care as much as you think. It's a job for them. I try to tell my mother this, but she doesn't listen."

(Child A)

"I love my parents. My mother and father talk about the value of education all the time. Fortunately, they make sure that I attend good schools. I have always had good teachers. They are smart and care about the students. My peers also seem to care about education. All of my friends plan to attend college and get good jobs. I must admit that although school is challenging, it is fun."

(Child B)

I would argue that children who fail in school do so in large part because they have not first established meaningful relationships with their parents.

Their parents have not prepared them educationally and socially. These same parents often abdicate their educational responsibilities to the school system. This could be a major error that profoundly influences how their children will perform and interact in school environments, particularly with adults. There may have been a brief time in history when parents could drop their children, problems and all, at the schoolhouse door. The schools seemed equipped to handle minor disciplinary issues, but times have changed. Parents (often single-parent households in urban centers) often have serious problems raising their children. If children are not disciplined in the home, they will likely behave in unruly fashion in school. From my professional experience, parents become reluctant partners with school staff because they believe school staff blames them for not being able to appropriately discipline or control their children's behavior at home and in school.

Another phenomenon worth noting is that the role of the father in a child's school experience has largely disappeared. Some mothers have been too often forced to assume the role of raising their children single-handedly. Even in families with both parents present, the father is too often the reluctant participant. This can leave the mother to fend for herself when she engages with school officials. I have observed school officials bullying parents. They do this by double- and triple-teaming mothers when they visit the school to talk about their children's behavior. Again, too many parents become weary and eventually stop engaging with the school staff.

I surmise that one strategy to address educational failure is to begin with training parents to network with other parents, school officials, and community stakeholders to support their children educationally. Children are not likely to succeed in schools without parents playing a critical role at home. Schools cannot function in isolation. They must work hand-in-hand with all stakeholders, particularly in urban communities. Parent and school partnerships are essential to a child's success in school (Epstein, 2001; Epstein, 2010).

Without this parent-school connection, school for many children becomes a necessary evil. Children who experience frequent failure attend school simply because they are told to attend, not because they want to attend. I believe if given a choice, the average child who drowns in school failure would opt to stay home and do absolutely nothing.

In addition to a parent-school connection, a parent-community partnership is critically important. Parents need the support of the community to help them raise their children. It really does take a community to raise children. It also takes a community to provide training and support for parents. I would argue that schools in urban centers fail largely because they fail to recognize the significance of school, family and community partnerships (Epstein, 2001; Epstein, 2010).

A quality education is one of the firmest pillars in a healthy community.
—*Bernard Gassaway*

School System Sanctioned Cheating: Credit Recovery

The teachers at John Dewey High School in New York City who anonymously reported credit recovery fraud should be applauded (Harris, 2015). Teachers and principals, like students, are victims of credit recovery and similar schemes. Credit recovery is a strategy that allows students to make up credits for courses that they have failed by completing makeup assignments.

I remember some time during my first two months as principal of Boys and Girls High School (BGHS) in 2009, I learned about credit recovery. Although I had served as an assistant principal of guidance at Far Rockaway High School (1994-1997) and as principal of Beach Channel High School (1997-2002), I never heard of credit recovery. This was a Bloomberg-Klein phenomenon.

After a brief investigation, I realized that credit recovery was a scheme to allow students to accumulate credits rapidly. This became an acceptable practice during my absence from the Department of Education (DOE) from 2005 to 2009. Rapid credit accumulation and extreme scrubbing of regents examinations were two methods used by school personnel to increase graduation rates.

School leaders leaped at the opportunity to show progress, almost at any cost. The unwritten rule was "Do it; just don't get caught."

I remember like it was yesterday when a student on one of our sports teams came to me in October 2009, two months after I began my tenure as principal of BGHS and gave me a folder with about five handouts in it. He said it was his credit recovery packet for art. I denied the student the credit. However, I did not blame him because he was taught that this practice was the norm. In fact, it was the norm.

It was at this point that I held an assembly program with the senior class.

With a microphone in hand, I said, "Effective immediately, credit recovery is dead at Boys and Girls High School!" In unison, approximately 400 seniors, 60% of them off track for graduation, yelled: "Boo! Boo! Boo! Boo!" One female student said, "F- that!" I ordered the dean to put her out of the auditorium while I regained control of the assembly. The students were furious. They were shocked. I did not expect such a vociferous reaction. I had hit a nerve. Some students believed I betrayed them. Heretofore, credit recovery had provided them with hope and a way out.

After I had dismissed the students from the assembly, several remained. One student said, "Mr. Gassaway, you are right. Credit recovery is a joke. But what are we going to do now?" I said, naïvely, "Pass your classes." I soon learned it was deeper than that. The students had come to expect and, sadly, rely on shortcuts to falsely achieve success. They willingly accepted the unwritten contract of deception. School officials and teachers also willingly endorsed and participated in the deception.

On another occasion, in 2010, a student came to me to request a transfer to Murray Bertram High School. A fellow student who transferred to Bertram had told him he could earn 20 credits in less than a year. Shortly after hearing about this, I wanted to learn more about the program. I was curious. During a professional development activity in Staten Island, I met the principal of Murray Bertram. I asked her about her credit recovery program. When she described it, I said to myself that's crazy! She will get caught, perhaps. Eventually, she did get caught, or at least the DOE pretended to catch her. I say this because they knew all along what she was doing. Remember the golden rule. "Do it; just don't get caught!"

DOE officials are not interested in getting it right. They do not want to expose a culture of cheating, which definitely exists, particularly in lower-performing schools. Principals are pressured to show greater gains than expected based on student data. In turn, they pressure teachers. Teachers do not expose cheating for fear they will lose their jobs or be ostracized, which is highly likely.

Teachers and principals would be condemned rather than cheered for exposing cheating. Sadly, because of past actions, too many teachers and principals will carry a legacy of deception to their retirement and to their graves. I applaud those teachers and principals who resist the pressure to cheat and do the right thing for their students. There are many of them, unfortunately not enough to change the past and current culture of cheating in NYC public schools.

Darkness cannot drive out darkness; only light can do that. Hate cannot drive out hate; only love can do that.

—*Martin Luther King, Jr*

Politicians or Pimps: Does it Make a Difference for School Children?

When I was a preteen, my friends and I would dream of becoming two things when we grew up: pimps and convicts. This is what we saw, so this is what we wanted to become. Though I never achieved the distinct misguided honor of becoming a pimp, I did achieve juvenile delinquent status after numerous encounters with law officials. Fortunately, through divine intervention, I overcame my blindness and began to see the light.

In light of recent events involving politicians across this country, from bribery convictions to alleged corruption of federal, state, and local elected officials, and to New York City Council members creating *dummy organizations* and misappropriating funds, I can't help but ask, "Are we the people being pimped by our politicians? Are we blind to their actions and inactions?"

It is almost cliché to compare politicians to pimps. Yes, politicians like pimps prostitute their people, otherwise known as constituents. Yes, politicians like pimps, promise their people a brighter future if they continue to sacrifice today. Yes, politicians, like pimps, rely on the ignorance of their followers. Ignorance is a prerequisite to follow any person who has no moral compass. Yes, politicians like pimps believe that their followers appreciate a good beating every now and then. Somehow, an occasional beating is interpreted as a sign of affection. I sadly remember when one of my former high school students said to me, "I know my man loves me because he beats me."

Ironically, many politicians, particularly those who may now be comfortably and conveniently identified as *African-American or people of color*, serve today because many people fought and died yesteryear for their right to vote. Today's politicians are direct beneficiaries of rivers of blood that flowed throughout this country we know as the United States of America. This often brings me to what may best be described as a dilemma.

Although I understand and appreciate the sacrifice that my ancestors made to secure my right to vote, I find it virtually impossible to bring myself to vote for some of the putrid individuals who now run for elected office. I ask, "How can I allow myself to be pimped by anyone?" I recognize the game, because the images and actions of pimp life are embedded in my psyche.

Of course, there are those politicians, Black, White and in between, who sacrifice for all people. The actions of their colleagues, however, often taint them.

I advise principals to develop purposeful partnerships with well-meaning politicians. Such politicians might be able to provide your school with needed resources. Monitor their moral compass while monitoring your own. Be careful not to make a deal with ill-meaning politicians. Many politicians are interested in reciprocal relationships. You may notice some may vote against the majority simply to curry a future vote for their own projects. Many refer to this as a political dance or quid pro quo. I call it selling your soul or selling your people, or simply pimping.

While politicians solicit unions for votes, let's remember that schools in their districts are failing children. They cannot boast about progress when children are being left behind. One of the most influential politicians in this country represents a NYC school district that has the largest number of failing schools. This is not new. It was this way when he entered office, and it will be that way when he leaves. Sadly, of all of his political capital, none of it was used to improve education for his constituents' children. Why? He and his colleagues are not doing anything to change the status quo.

To be fair, I must acknowledge that *politician* is a word or noun that should not be reserved for elected officials. A large number of community-based organizations are run by politicians of a different stripe, de facto or surrogate politicians. What makes them different? Is it that they are politicians for hire? No. What makes them different is that it is not illegal to pay for their influence.

It is imperative that principals and other school officials be ever mindful of their moral compass when dealing with politicians. Keep the focus on the children. They, not you or politicians, should be the ones to benefit from your relationships and partnerships.

He who opens a school door, closes a prison.

—*Victor Hugo*

School-to-Prison Pipeline: A By-product of Educational Inequity

When John woke up this morning to get ready for school, he never imagined that he would spend the night in the local juvenile detention center for cursing at a teacher who had asked him to go to class. The fact that John was robbed and beaten by a group of teens on his way to school did not factor into the principal's decision to have the school safety agent arrest him for disorderly conduct. No one bothered to ask John why he was angry or to refer him to a counselor. As a consequence of being arrested in school, John joined a growing fraternity of young students who have experienced the school-to-prison pipeline.

The school-to-prison pipeline is predominantly an urban phenomenon. Children are pushed through the pipeline by public school administrators who are prone to suspend students or call the police to arrest them for minor infractions (Hall & Karanxha, 2012; Herbert, 2007). Underfunded schools are not appropriately staffed to address the needs of students who are often described as having behavioral problems, being under-credited and over-aged, marginalized, or at-risk. The least expensive option is to push out troubled students by having them arrested or drop out (Kim, Losen, & Hewitt, 2010). Once they are labeled and classified, school failure becomes more predictable. Under the zero-tolerance policy, these students are likely candidates for future incarceration (Hall & Karanxha, 2012; Herbert, 2007; Sullivan, 2007).

This unfortunate reality can be directly attributed to educational inequity. It is not a leap to connect high dropout rates and high incarceration rates to a poor educational system. When children are poorly educated, they are more likely to go to prison than to college (Harlow, 2003; Kim,

Losen, & Hewitt, 2010; Lee et al., 2007, Mitra, 2011; Spangenberg, 2004; Stephens as cited in Vacca, 2004; Sum et al., 2009).

Children who grow up to face time in prison are often part of communities that have not invested in education (Kim, Losen, & Hewitt, 2010; Mitra, 2011). In far too many cases, this means that quality guidance counseling services are not available for these children (Bryant, 2015; Sullivan, 2007). While school officials in underfunded schools may be able to identify the problems children have, unfortunately, they lack the resources to do anything about them. Consequently, many of these children may become wards of the criminal justice system.

I offer the following recommendations to stem the tide of children going through the school-to-prison pipeline:

- Invest in education. This means recruit the best teachers to work with children who have a history of educational discrimination vis-à-vis inequitable funding. Build state-of-the-art schools and community centers. Provide ongoing training to teachers. Remove incompetent teachers from the teaching ranks.
- Close the school-to-prison pipeline while simultaneously expanding and improving the prison-to-school pipeline. Provide funding for state-of-the-art vocational, academic, and career guidance programs and facilities for inmates while they are in prison (Davis et al., 2014; Gordon & Weldon, 2003; Vernick & Reardon, 2001). Do not relegate prison-school space to the darkest dungeon-like areas of the prisons or provide only obsolete equipment and material. Paradoxically, the prison-to-school pipeline may be the lifeline that brings about hope to the hopeless. The proverbial light bulb may shine brightly in the darkest places.
- Amend current federal and state policies that make it virtually impossible for a person with a felony conviction to acquire a government loan to attend college or work in certain professions. These policies send a clear message that it is nearly impossible to pay a debt to society. Like Prometheus, one's sentence and

punishment may be eternal. We must change this stance. Each prison sentence need not be a death sentence or eternal damnation. By limiting the options for formerly incarcerated people, we increase the likelihood of their imminent return to prison. This is socially and morally reprehensible.

- Develop accountability standards for correctional education programs. Officials need to identify better ways to evaluate prison-based programs (Davis et al., 2014; Wade, 2007). The absence of standards makes it difficult to determine if programs work.
- Provide drug and alcohol treatment to inmates while they are incarcerated. Education alone will not adequately meet the needs of inmates, many who come to prison with a plethora of social deficits (Davis et al., 2014; Ismailova, 2007; Steurer, Smith & Tracey, 2001).
- Establish partnerships between correctional education programs, community-based organizations and colleges. These partnerships could provide inmates with a seamless transition from prison education and career guidance programs to community-based programs. Getting Out, Staying Out; The Fortune Society; and New York City's CUNY Catch are examples of model programs.
- Develop best practices in correctional education. This would require researchers, educators, practitioners and policymakers to work together to develop best practices for correctional education programs (Davis et al., 2014; LoBuglio, 2005; Vernick & Reardon, 2001). Currently, many prisons—namely federal, state, and local—are working as independent entities in this regard.
- Support legislation that provide inmates post-release with improved access to employment and healthcare, including drug and alcohol treatment and housing. Along with education, these are the pillars necessary to sustain viability and maintain freedom. The social amenities and skill needs of individuals before they go to prison are the same and sometimes greater when they

are released from prison: education, employment, housing and healthcare.

- Recruit, reward and train educators who choose to work in prisons. Good teachers make a difference irrespective of the working environment. I have witnessed the care and compassion of educators who teach in prisons. They choose to work with individuals who are incarcerated for many reasons. Mainly they care and see potential in individuals who may have been written off by others. Interestingly, prison-based educators themselves are in de facto prisons albeit for a 6- to 8-hour workday. Their working conditions are usually not optimal (Sarra & Olcott, 2007). Nevertheless, many of them perform a commendable service to society.

A Parent's Cry for Help: A Case for Collaboration, not Condemnation

School leaders need to rethink how they relate to parents. Parents need to be trained how to interact with school personnel. School officials claim that they value parent involvement. Yet, they cannot clearly articulate their own vision for involvement. Conversely, parents say they want to be informed by school officials when their children are not making the grade. Yet, when they receive frequent calls, parents become annoyed at the school personnel.

One day I received a call from a parent. She was annoyed at how the school official handled notifying her about her son's truancy. Before she could explain all that she had done to get her child to attend school regularly, including subtle forms of bribery, the official threatened to report her for parental neglect. This parent needed the school official to help her, not humiliate her.

In working with parents to navigate the school system, I have concluded that school officials should rethink how they relate to parents, rather than focusing on how parents should relate to them. If parents had a magic wand to change their children and make them perfect students, I am sure they would use it. However, there is no magic wand to help parents' troubled children.

Watching parents interact within school systems reminds me of when my mother visited my school 45 years ago. It was only when I became a teacher that I could appreciate what my mother had to endure with me. My mother did not like going to the school. I am certain now that she was embarrassed and felt vulnerable. After some 40 to 50 visits on account of my behavioral issues, she developed a fear of interacting with school staff. The school staff refused to help my mother and basically told her, "Bernard is bad. Make him change his behavior." My mother tried, as many parents try with their children, with varying degrees of success.

When parents lack the skills to make their children "good," the school staff should not continue with the same approach. "Your child is bad. Make him good." Some schools go further and say, "Make him good or else we will put him in special education or call the child protection agency to report parental neglect." This type of threat by school officials is unacceptable. Unfortunately, they do it and get away with it. Regardless of how "bad" children may behave, it is never easy for parents to accept criticism of their children. School personnel need to care about how they deal with parents—informing parents of their children's behavior is not enough. Parents need to be helped to develop strategies to improve their relationship with their children.

On one occasion, I accompanied a parent to a meeting to discuss with school personnel what, if any, special education services should be provided to the child. The staff had taken the position that the child should be placed in a restrictive, self-contained environment. From what I knew about the case, there was no clear justification for this position. The parent was adamantly opposed to any change in her child's program. The school attempted to persuade her. They brought in the child's teachers to discuss her performance. The parent and I listened. At any given time, there were five staff members in the meeting: two teachers, a school psychologist, a social worker, and an assistant principal. None of the school staff was aware of my professional background. I did not identify my credentials until the meeting concluded. What disturbed the parent and me was that the psychologist and social worker tag-teamed in a way that confused and disempowered the parent. They spoke continuously and simultaneously. There was no way the parent could understand them. I, however, understood the jargon they used. At the end of the meeting I said, "What just happened was not right. You spoke too fast and at the same time. How do you expect parents to understand their rights?" When I explained that I was a former teacher, principal, and superintendent, they looked surprised, as if they had been caught doing something wrong. They apologized. I wondered how often they had repeated their act with unprepared parents.

Caring school personnel should understand that when parents are summoned to the school to discuss their child's performance, they become defensive. Parents, and especially mothers, instinctively want to protect their young. School personnel need to be trained to welcome parents, regardless of the reason they are being called to the school. I know from personal experience that school officials travel in numbers. When they meet with parents, they usually outnumber them. That is intimidating. School staff speak a different language. Parents are self-conscious about their appearance and worry about how they sound. They do not want to sound unintelligent. Their children are apprehensive for the same reasons. Parents feel judged before they arrive at the school. "School officials must think I am a bad parent because of the way my child behaves." Sure there are parents who believe their children can do no wrong. While it is difficult to work with these parents, school personnel should nevertheless come prepared to be supportive and to recommend ways to collaborate with the parents to improve the child's behavior and performance.

Powerful people cannot afford to educate the people that they oppress, because once you are truly educated, you will not ask for power. You will take it.

—*John Henrik Clarke*

Action Plan for Parents: Parents, Mind Your Own Business

The following is excerpted from one of my articles, "Parents, Mind Your Own Business." Parents and school personnel may be able to use some of these recommendations to improve parent-school relations.

School business is for educators, not parents. Parents need to focus more on raising their children than getting too involved in what goes on in schools.

As harsh as this may sound, this is an expressed sentiment among many educators across this country in both public and private school systems. I have heard this from colleagues, and I have experienced it as a parent.

Disconnected, Disrespected and Dismissed

Parents, in overwhelming numbers, you have expressed feeling disconnected, disrespected and dismissed by New York City Department of Education (DOE) officials. This happens for numerous reasons.

DOE officials rely on your lack of unity. Time and time again they see how easy it is to manipulate you.

They spread rumors to weaken any bonds that may exist among you. They infiltrate your organizations.

They make under-the-table deals with individuals and community-based organizations to influence your decisions and actions. Since they do not respect you, they will use anyone, even your children, to get their way—a way that is often not in the best interest of your children.

DOE officials rely on your lack of stamina. They are practically immune to the occasional protests held at city hall or DOE headquarters.

Once the protest is over, they expect you to disperse and go away. An effective protest should last as long as necessary to achieve its goal. If officials are not inconvenienced in any measurable way, they do not care if you protest.

DOE officials rely on your blind faith. You turn your child over to them for approximately two hundred days per year, six hours per day. Yet, you spend less than two hours in the school all year. You believe in their evaluation of your child, in most cases without question. You know very little about the counselors, teachers and administrators, who are responsible for your child's physical and mental well-being.

DOE officials rely on your fear. You fear their dominance and deprecation. You fear their retribution and retaliation. You fear their arrogance and authority. They serve as judge, jury and executioner. You and your child are at their mercy.

DOE officials rely on your lack of options. They readily dismiss you because you have limited options.

Private school is not an option for many. They realize the majority of families whose children attend public school fall below the poverty line and can barely afford to pay for living expenses, let alone pay for an education.

Strategies for Effective Engagement with School Officials

1. Listen. Tune into what your child says about the quality of his teachers. Children are often accurate. Schools that serve poor, Latino and Black children have a disproportionate number of unqualified teachers. If your child has unqualified teachers, fight to have his classes or school changed. Your engagement with school officials begins with your child.
2. Praise, honor and support good teachers. Tell and show them how much you appreciate what they are doing for your child.
3. Seek support. Do not suffer in silence. Find other parents who have experienced what you are going through. They may be able to help you resolve your issues.
4. Plan for meetings with school personnel. Never meet with them

alone. Bring people, your pastor, friends, and family members. There is strength in numbers.
5. Deliberate. Take a reasonable amount of time to think about any school-related decisions. Do not allow school officials to pressure you into making rash decisions. Confer with family, clergy or parent/child advocates.
6. Attend and participate in school-related activities. Share your opinion. Volunteer. The staff should know you as a concerned and involved parent. When they know and respect you, they are more likely to know and respect your child. Likewise, when your child knows you are involved, he is more likely to behave and perform well.

Things You Should Expect from the School System:

1. Request a copy of your child's school records. You have a right to any material in her official file. This is extremely important. You need to know what is being documented about your child and in some cases, what may be said about you, as a parent. Read the contents of the file with your child.
2. Visit your child's class during school hours. Give at least one day's notice. You must avoid disruption. You should not attempt to speak with the teacher during this visit. Ask for a tour of the school. Your purpose is to observe the lesson, class and school climate.
3. Schedule appointments to meet with your child's teachers. Do not wait until the bi-annual parent-teacher conferences. Prepare specific questions before the meeting. Meetings may be scheduled for after regular school hours. This may allow for meaningful discussions and fewer interruptions.
4. Volunteer to work in the parent office. Each school should have at least one office dedicated to parents. Parent-friendly schools will have Parent Reception or Resource Centers that are accessible during and after the regular school day.

5. Ensure school personnel are able to contact you. It is your responsibility to inform them when your contact information changes. You should not place this responsibility on your child.
6. Meet with appropriate school personnel to deal with concerns. Decide if it is necessary to meet the principal in order to get your matter resolved. Though the principal should be accessible to parents, it may not be possible to meet her immediately. You may expedite the resolution if you target the person who will ultimately be able to help you directly.
7. Attend workshops for parents. Parent-friendly schools offer them regularly. These may include computer training, reading, writing, math, music, art and others.
8. Attend school assembly programs that honor children. You may need to take a day or a few hours off from work. Programs may also be held on weekends and evenings. You should attend with your child even if she is not being honored. It may serve as a motivation for you and her while simultaneously showing support for other children and families.

Parents, Know Your Business

1. Meet with your child at the beginning of each school year. Discuss what he is expected to learn in and out of school.
2. Monitor your child's development. Do not rely on school tests to define your child's level of intelligence. Focus on whether he is acquiring life skills. How would he respond to unanticipated occurrences? Do you see and hear him thinking?
3. Seek help for your child through local libraries, community organizations, churches and nontraditional institutions. Consider peer tutoring as an option. It is an overlooked effective strategy.
4. Schedule meaningful activities for your child. These may include family trips to the park, museum, library, neighborhood walks, and volunteering at a local food pantry or shelter. Idle time for an

active child is asking for trouble. Keep your child busy. Keep him physically, mentally and culturally engaged.
5. Stay active in your child's life. Children with active parents are less likely to be abused by school personnel. Child predators try to avoid the kind of attention involved parents bring.
6. Train your child to think. This does not happen in traditional schools. They train your child to pass tests. They train your child to conform. The school system discourages differences and independence. Children with independent spirits generally do not function well in school without involved parents. Children who learn differently are often labeled and neglected. They are punished or dispirited by a system that mandates uniformity and conformity.
7. Make certain your child's educational needs are met. Be a squeaky wheel. School officials do not expect you to be persistent. Call, write and visit daily if necessary. If the system labels or harms your child, make them pay for it. Seek legal counsel and take them to court. Charge them with educational neglect, deprivation and malfeasance.

Conclusion

A tidal wave begins with a ripple. You serve as a ripple in your child's life. Join with other ripples (including committed and concerned school personnel) and make waves. When parents, community and school personnel are on the same page, working together, children thrive.

Book III

I have never let my education interfere with my education.

—*Mark Twain*

Choices

As a leader, I attempted to surround myself with individuals who would exercise independent thinking. I wanted to be challenged. I wanted to hear and examine all sides of a position or argument. This approach seemed to work well for me. I prepared for policy meetings as debaters prepared for major debates. You need to know both sides of the argument. This involves having the ability to listen to people. Consult with them. People may not always agree with your final decision, but they might respect how you made it.

Leadership in Practice: Decision-making

During my tenure as senior superintendent of alternative schools and programs (2003-2005), I was responsible for running various General Equivalency Diploma (GED) programs. I believed the New York City Department of Education's (DOE) GED program was not meeting the needs of the students. High schools would routinely refer over-age and under-credited students to GED programs without regard to their reading and math levels. As a result, many of these students would drop out of the GED program. In essence, these students were being pushed out of the public school system.

For instance, principals, deans, and guidance counselors would encourage students who frequently fought, cut, were absent, or failed to earn course credits, to transfer into GED programs. These programs provided school personnel with a way to push out students who were not performing to standard or were causing problems for the staff. In essence, the GED programs were used as a "dumping ground" for students, a phrase I use reluctantly. The mere description of "dumping" connotes garbage—an association that should not be made when referring to students, regardless of how poorly they may have behaved. Unfortunately, the GED program was seen as a place to banish students rather than as a viable educational option.

Ideally, on average, a student needed to function on seventh grade reading and math levels to be a viable candidate for the GED program. In order to accommodate the large number of students being forced out of traditional schools, the alternative district eliminated academic requirements for enrolling in a GED program. As a result, the floodgates opened. High school students reading two to three years below grade level were being referred to GED programs. They were being told by staff to leave their home school to get a GED. It was pitched to them as a quicker way to attain a diploma and to attend college.

Significant Decision

There are numerous GED programs in New York City. Some of the programs are operated by private, public and not-for-profit organizations. The largest GED program in the DOE was called Auxiliary Services for High Schools (ASHS). They began each school year with an average register of approximately 14,000 students. The student register would be used to determine their budget. They operated 51 day and evening sites throughout the five boroughs of New York City. They served adolescents and adults. After my staff and I closely analyzed the data and visited all of the sites, we determined that the program needed to be reformed. After consulting all of the stakeholders, including community-based organizations, students, teachers, teacher's union, central personnel, and parents, we decided that reform was the correct course of action. However, the stakeholders could not agree on what sites should be closed or reorganized.

As senior superintendent, I (based on my team's analysis) had to decide whether to maintain the 51 sites or restructure the program, which would result in closing the majority of sites, since they had low enrollments and were failing.

Data

On average, 7,000 students would be discharged as dropouts from ASHS. Of the 7,000 remaining students, approximately 2,500 would earn GEDs. The following school term, the enrollment at ASHS would again rise to 14,000 students. Annually 20% to 30% of the GED candidates would pass the examination. In some sites, 60% to 80% of the students would drop out of the program. This cycle was repeated year after year, as a result of the tendency among traditional high schools to push out a greater number of students.

Substantive Information

We acknowledged in our analysis that the GED program often fought an uphill battle. Nevertheless, a culture of failure could not be acceptable. Here is what we knew:

- Students were not attending the GED programs (40% average daily attendance).
- Administrators (citywide) were inappropriately referring students to GED programs.
- The GED program (ASHS in particular) continued to expand in students and personnel.
- Nearly 80% of the students would eventually drop out.
- The number of functionally illiterate students being referred to GED programs increased significantly.
- Student morale was extremely low.
- Staff morale was extremely low.
- A culture of failure was prevalent throughout the program.

Time for a Change

When we decided as a district to focus on reforming the GED program, we knew we would receive pushback. We did not know how much. After months of analysis and meetings with all of the major stakeholders, we decided that many of the GED sites should be closed. This decision was based on the fact that the average daily attendance at these sites was only 40%, and even lower at other sites. Furthermore, and frankly, these sites remained open more for political than academic reasons. GED programs provided jobs.

These changes meant that staff would be reassigned. The union did not strongly object to this reform. Their only concern was that teachers not be fired. This could not happen for contractual reasons. Arguably, some of the teachers should never have been hired to teach children.

Recommendations

Based on information gathered from numerous consultation meetings, one-on-one meetings with various stakeholders and research on best practices, we compiled and considered the following recommendations:

- Establish community-based organizations (CBO) partnerships with each GED site.
- Develop a coherent professional development series for GED administrative and pedagogical staff to raise the level of instruction and infuse youth development strategies.
- Close sites that are not meeting the academic standards as well as the developmental needs of the students.
- Evaluate GED programs to incorporate career and technical education and information pertaining to college opportunities.
- Change the current practice that allows ASHS to serve students over 21 years of age.
- Establish distance learning programs for high-school-age GED candidates.
- Enable students to earn course credits that will allow them to transition back to a diploma granting institution.

Decision and Ramifications

After consulting with parents, students, teachers, administrators and central personnel we decided to close the majority of the GED sites. The new plan called for eleven day sites and five evening sites to remain operational. This took us from 51 sites to a total of 16. After visiting nearly 90% of the sites, I witnessed poor instruction, low attendance and staff apathy. I expected political fallout. What I didn't expect was the alacrity with which DOE central leadership retreated from our plan once they faced the first wave of opposition. I say "our plan" because they were completely involved in its development. They—the special assistant to the chancellor and others—had given tacit approval of the plan. The moment the New

York Times and channel 7 Eyewitness News aired the story, DOE officials told me to reopen additional sites, even though they knew these sites had failed children for years. It had no foundation in sound pedagogy. It was purely a political decision.

On September 30, 2004, the *New York Times* headline read, "Help Centers for Dropouts Are Closed." The article went on to say,

> The New York City Education Department has shut down dozens of sites used by dropouts to prepare for the high school equivalency exam, bewildering staff members and creating a chaotic situation for young people already at risk of abandoning their studies.
>
> Mr. Gassaway, the senior superintendent, said officials decided to consolidate the auxiliary services program because most of those students were not being served well—less than 20% of those enrolled earned high school equivalency degrees last year. And, according to the Education Department, the four-year dropout rates at auxiliary programs last year ranged from 66% in Queens to 80% in the Bronx.

I, and others, knew firsthand that students' instructional needs were not being addressed by these programs. I also knew that any attempt to reorganize the programs would be met with fierce resistance. I felt morally obligated to do the right thing, regardless of the outcome and how it may have affected my career. Not once did I waiver for fear of retribution. In the face of great opposition, DOE central personnel distanced themselves from our decision, caved in and reopened some of the closed programs. They admitted to me privately that what we did (as a district) was probably the right thing to do, even though it may not have been politically feasible.

I reluctantly opened five additional evening sites and four day sites.

Reflection

The standards movement created conditions whereby truly at-risk students were only given the option of earning a GED. Sadly, some students were targeted and tracked for GED as early as the eighth grade. When a student did not show progress or misbehaved in class, there were generally three pathways available: special education, GED placement or extrication (push out).

I felt strongly that the GED phenomenon was an intra-system problem. Administrators throughout the system passed the proverbial buck. If they were intolerant with a student, they simply passed him or her on to the next school. This was not unlike the practice of passing poorly performing teachers to schools to get the teacher out of one's building. "Good luck to the sucker who gets you!" Seeking an alternative for children is not necessarily a bad thing; the goal and the challenge is to be thoughtful about the alternative and to ensure that the proposed placement is appropriate.

There was no evidence that children were harmed by the decision to restructure the largest GED program in New York. We established additional literacy centers to address the needs of the students who were inappropriately placed in GED programs. We improved professional development for the staff. We established partnerships with universities and colleges, notably Fordham University.

I remained superintendent for one year after the restructuring. Some progress was noted. However, more time would be required for sites to develop identity and culture.

With the benefit of hindsight, I would make the same decision today. The controversy was political in nature. Politics will surface whenever people have hidden agendas. In this case, the hidden agenda was job comfort and security, not what was best for the students. You see, no teachers were ever in danger of losing their jobs.

Prison-to-School Pipeline: Reversal of Misfortunes

What happens when children are not educated adequately? What happens when they drop out, or are forced out, of school? Some might answer, "They may end up in prison." For far too many young people, school serves as a direct pipeline to prison, particularly in poor urban school districts.

Having been an educator for more than 25 years in New York City (NYC), I have seen too many teenagers become involved in the criminal justice system. Some were arrested while attending school. Others were arrested after they had dropped out or after their schools pushed them out.

This subject is important to me because as a teenager I was also entangled in the criminal justice system. Fortunately, as a result of positive relationships and interventions, I was able to change my destructive path. I was enrolled in educational programs where adults cared about me. This played a significant role in my social development and later success.

When I served as the superintendent of alternative schools and programs in NYC, I supervised school programs at juvenile and adult detention facilities. During a visit to one of these facilities, I overheard a teacher say to a student detainee, "Make sure you do not come back once you get out." I asked myself, "If nothing changes for him during his period of incarceration, what would prevent him from coming back?" I then asked myself, "What would happen if we reversed the school-to-prison pipeline?" A significant intervention for inmates might be providing them with access to good academic and vocational programs, thus cultivating a *prison-to-school* pipeline.

On one particularly cold, wintry morning, I sat in the makeshift auditorium at NYC's Rikers Island, one of the country's largest municipal jails. As I waited to be introduced to speak to approximately 100 student-inmates as a guest of their Black History program, I thought about a conference on educational equity scheduled to take place at Teachers College on the same day. I wondered what would be said at the conference that would affect these and other students who might be headed to jail, partly as a consequence of educational inequity. I also wondered if the goal of educational equity included these student-inmates at all.

Some of the student-inmates I spoke to at the assembly program immediately returned to society. Others began a term of incarceration in a state or federal prison. When they arrived at their destination, apart from the expected fight for survival due to the harsh realities of prison life, including gangs, violence, degradation and humiliation, few educational services were available for them, particularly if they were over 21. According to various sources, the availability and quality of services varies from state to state. Federal prisons seem to provide the highest level of services (Spangenberg, 2004). This means that inmates' access to adequate educational services would depend largely on where they were placed (Clarke, 2014; Davis et al., 2014). Additionally, because of a lack of uniform standards of education and accountability across private, state and federal prisons, not much is known about the quality of the services being offered (Coley & Barton, 2006). We only know that funding for prison-based education varies state to state (Clarke, 2014).

The student-inmates assembled for the Black History program were able to attend a prison-based school during incarceration because of the Handberry litigation (Handberry v. Thompson, 1996). This school, Horizon Academy, was opened in 1998 to redress the wrongs outlined in the lawsuit. During my tenure as senior superintendent of New York City's alternative schools, responsible for oversight of the educational programs on Rikers Island from 2003 to 2005, I learned that these programs had not received enough funding. If traditional schools were underfunded by New York State's educational funding formulas, as proven in litigation by the Campaign for Fiscal Equity case *CFE v. New York State*, prison education programs received a pittance.

We must ask ourselves, once these children land in prison, should they be denied an adequate education? Cases like *Handberry* made the argument that inmates who are between 16 and 21 years old have a constitutional right to an adequate education, even during their period of incarceration. What happens when inmates are older than 21? Does the state have an ethical obligation to extend educational services to inmates beyond 21, given evidence that they were denied an adequate education prior to turning 21? I would argue that there should be no statute of limitation to redress wrongs wrought by educational inequity.

It should never be too late to redress a wrong. Access to a relevant and adequate education should be afforded to all who have been denied it, regardless of how long it takes.

Who Pays the Price for Educational Inequity?

We may ask: Does society benefit from continuing to deny individuals an adequate education once they are incarcerated, particularly if it can be shown that education increases the likelihood of rehabilitation and successful reentry into society (Davis et al., 2014)?

Here's what we have learned about prisoners who lack education. We know from available studies that nearly 70% of inmates who leave prison are likely to be rearrested or return to prison within three years of their release. Coincidentally, we also know that a high percentage of inmates in prison dropped out of school (Davis et al., 2014; Lee et al., 2007; Sum et al., 2009; U.S. Bureau of Justice Statistics, 2002; Vacca, 2004).

According to a large body of research, recidivism rates decrease when inmates participate in education programs while in prison, especially when compared to inmates who choose not to participate (Davis et al., 2014; Ismailova, 2007; Nuttall, Hollmen & Staley, 2003; Vacca, 2004). Since policymakers and practitioners are probably aware of these findings, why hasn't there been a concerted push for greater investment in prison education programs? This is our current challenge.

Some might respond that the penal system is not in the business of improving education or reducing recidivism. Its role is to house, control and punish inmates. We do know that without opportunities for education, housing, healthcare, and employment, formerly incarcerated individuals are likely to commit future crimes and return to prison (Spangenberg, 2004). Surely, this cycle of incarceration would be both socially and financially costly.

We can learn from available evidence that the greater good of society may be to provide inmates with opportunities to receive quality educational services while incarcerated. It is indeed ironic that in too many cases these same services may have been denied to them when they were physically free. In other cases, they may not have been ready to receive the available services.

Ultimately, society pays the price for educational inequity.

Million Dollar Teachers: It's Time for Change

For several years I have given a great deal of thought to what it would take to make urban school systems in the U.S. work for all children. The answer hit me early one Sunday morning. We must rid school systems of ineffective teachers and pay effective teachers higher salaries. So, I said to myself, why not pay teachers as we pay professional athletes—millions of dollars based on their value as educational players?

People around the world never thought they would see the day when a Colored, Negro, Black, or African-American, would be elected president of the United States of America. I believe the same is true of education: *"I will never see the day when urban schools in America will work for all children."*

Imagine waking up one morning to read the following headline in your local newspaper: A NEW YORK CITY SCHOOL DISTRICT AGREES TO PAY TEACHERS AT HOPE ACADEMY SALARIES IN EXCESS OF $1 MILLION. Teachers have agreed to the following conditions: They pledge first, never to turn away or discharge children for academic, social, or behavioral reasons; second, they pledge to identify and help remove teachers who are unwilling and unable to teach children; third, they pledge to tie their salaries and job security to student outcomes, as measured by multiple forms of assessments, including peer and independent review, and portfolio and lesson observations. The teachers' union also pledges to work with the school district to purge the system of unwilling and unable teachers. It is also working with colleges and universities to recruit the future stars of the teaching profession. The ultimate goal is to ensure that every child has the opportunity for an adequate education. This, at the very least, would require that students have teachers who teach effectively and obtain good results.

Educational insiders know that school reform will not work unless the issue of teacher quality/effectiveness is confronted head-on. Here is what I recommend: Draft teachers as professional sports teams draft athletes. What will this accomplish? The best teachers with a proven history of teaching all children will get paid to work with a team of other highly qualified "players" to compete to win the coveted prize of motivating children to succeed.

To further this analogy, there would be no farm league where teachers can practice or experiment on live "subjects," as is currently happening across America's urban educational landscape. Weak and fledgling teachers will no longer be allowed to find refuge in urban schools that mainly serve poor and disenfranchised children, something we know would not likely be allowed to happen in wealthier communities without consequences.

When I was a high school principal in an urban area, one of the most difficult decisions I had to make was to program children to classes where I knew the teacher was not highly effective. Frankly, in some cases, I questioned and challenged the system that hired the teacher. My worse days were when a student forced me to suspend disbelief by asking or begging me to transfer him or her from a teacher's class because the teacher was "not teaching." At times I felt powerless, because I was unable to remove the teacher from the school if he or she met the minimum requirements set by the state. This did not absolve me from having to make an ethical decision. So, I would often grant the transfer request; however, what pained me was that I knew I had left others behind. In a perfect world, the teacher in this case would be receptive to professional development. Unfortunately, the challenge for many urban school administrators is that teachers too often do not see a problem with their pedagogy. When confronted, they seem dumbfounded by any constructive criticism. Until we are able to overcome the barrier of Cartesian self-delusion ("I think I am a great teacher, therefore I am") too many children will not learn. Very few efforts at school reform really get to the heart of what needs to be reformed. When you improve teacher quality, you improve educational opportunities for children.

Once, during a trip to the Central Park Zoo, a volunteer introduced me to the chevrotain, or mouse deer. She said that the species had not changed in over 30 million years. It was never forced by its environment to change. Immediately, I made a parallel connection to school teachers in America. I said,

"They, like the chevrotain, have not been forced to change by their environment." In many ways, teachers' unions protect teachers from change. Examine school reforms across this country and ask how many of them have successfully influenced teacher quality? Michele Rehee, former Chancellor of District of Columbia Public Schools, attempted to get teachers to give up tenure for higher compensation. She was unable to persuade teachers to change the way they see and do their jobs—something that has not happened since as far back as when Dewey and Mann helped lay the foundation for education in this country.

Paying our highly qualified teachers million-dollar salaries might be the key to real reform. Good, hard-working, qualified teachers need an incentive to purge their profession of weak and incompetent teachers. Money may be what it takes to change a union that represents the good and the bad. Unions should not protect the bad in order to maintain the right to protect the good. (I borrowed the language "good" and "bad" from teacher parlance, as many of them describe students using these adjectives.)

In conclusion, as long as the interests of adults compete against the interests of children, children lose. Paying teachers' salaries in excess of a million dollars may be the thing to reverse the natural principle of self-preservation—within the world of education we need to establish the principle of student preservation. This principle means teachers can survive only when students survive or achieve. There must be a realization that teachers' destinies should be inextricably connected to students' destinies. Our education system will continue to fail as long as teachers are rewarded even when children are not given adequate opportunities to learn.

Fathers: Unwelcomed in Urban Schools

As a former school official, I can recount almost all of the encounters I had with fathers in schools. There were few. Interestingly, when I did deal with fathers, they were effective in working with their children. Rarely—if ever—did a father say to me, I do not know what to do with my child. The problem is that far too many single-parent households are led by mothers who were essentially abandoned by their men to raise the children on their own. The effects of this burden are acutely evident in schools across this country.

The relative absence of fathers from the schoolhouse doors probably cuts across all racial and ethnic groups. I can only speak to what has been my experience in public education. I have worked in de facto segregated and integrated schools. Fathers were relatively absent in both. My best experience with fathers came during my tenure as principal of Beach Channel High School. The Reverend Henry Maddox was the PTA president and later co-president with his wife, Reverend Lucille Maddox. I have said before that my experience as a principal would have been a total disaster had it not been for these two individuals. They were my partners. I listened to them and valued their advice and counsel. Henry Maddox was a strong man. I embraced his strength.

I honestly believe that some school leaders prefer that fathers remain behind the scenes or out of the schools. On the one hand, school officials want both parents to be involved in their children's education. On the other hand, they prefer working directly with the mother. Why? We live in a sexist society. Some male school officials attempt to take advantage of female parents. Think of your own experience dealing with school personnel. I am reminded of a principal in Queens, New York who seems to take pleasure in verbally abusing the Parents Association Officers—all women.

He does it because he gets away with it. He has shown little respect for women. I have observed how he relates to men. He becomes demure and reserved, even deferential. It's a physical and psychological phenomenon that is hardly discussed in educational circles. This would be a good area for empirical research.

Legal Tightrope

I can recall countless times when mothers would leave specific instructions with the school not to allow contact between children and their fathers. This included denying any requests for academically-related information. As school officials, we were in no position to advocate for the father because we had few if any details about the relationship between the parents. As school officials, we were pretty much bound by the dictates of the parent who enrolled the child. I cannot recall an instance when a father enrolled a child with specific instructions not to allow contact between the mother and the child—though I can imagine this happens.

Community Outreach

RISE, Inc., a community organization in Queens, sponsored several Real Men Read programs. This program basically invites men into the school on a particular day to read to the students. Each time it was a resounding success. RISE focused on boys. On this day, the school would separate boys and girls. The largely female staff welcomed the change in the school's dynamic for the day. There was, according to some, a noticeable positive difference in the way the boys behaved on these days and shortly thereafter.

In one school, I observed an interesting phenomenon. The male teachers seemed threatened by the presence of 'outsiders.' They essentially withdrew from participating in the event. Rather than help with the reading and organizing the event, they huddled in corners together as if to say, "Yo da man, do you!" It was sad to witness. Why would they be threatened if they were 'real men' throughout the year? No so-called outsider could 'take their place.' It was an amazing dynamic to watch. On other occasions, the male staff embraced the program and participated fully. This was magical!

Where Do We Go from Here?

If school personnel are to begin to deal with their failure to appropriately educate Black boys, they must overcome their fear of Black men.

I am not aware of any programs that train school officials how to welcome men into schools. I imagine there are some—surely, this would be the exception rather than the rule. For African-American men particularly, schools may not be welcoming environments. It is difficult for school officials to distinguish between Black men and Black boys. They generally border on treating them the same—disrespectfully. Interestingly, this treatment comes from Black and White school personnel, especially school safety agents. The Black man is perceived as a threat. That is just the way it is—a close examination of American history will bear this out.

Finally, we spend a lot of time trying to come up with substitutes for the family unit. The latest craze is male mentoring. A mentor cannot substitute a father. Unfortunately, this is how many programs are being marketed. Children need fathers in their lives. This message is directed at fathers, mothers, and school officials. A large part of community and educational failure is the breakdown of the family unit. Unless we determine ways to strengthen families, things may only get worse.

I freed a thousand slaves I could have freed a thousand more if only they knew they were slaves.

—*Harriet Tubman*

Action Plan for Community: An Open Letter to Black Clergy

Dear Pastors:

As leaders of the most powerful, respected and trusted institution in our communities, you have the ability to join forces to change the educational landscape for our children. It is clear that the public school system has failed poor and Black children. What is not clear is: How long will we allow this to happen?

As some public officials manipulate statistics to paint a brighter picture, the harsh reality is that too many of our children, despite structural reforms, continue to be denied a sound education. There is no viable action plan. City and state officials have not demonstrated ability or will to transform and improve the quality of education for all children. Of the numerous reforms in public education, none of them hit the core of the problem: institutional racism. An institution rooted in racist ideologies and practices will never completely meet the needs of poor and Black children. We cannot wait any longer.

Why we can't wait. We cannot wait because our children need us now. They are being undereducated. We are losing too many children to the streets, drugs and violence. Many have no dreams, no faith and no hope. We must not be afraid to ask the question: Why should we continue to wait for someone to do for us what we should and must do for ourselves?

Many of you do great things for children in your individual churches. I appeal to you to get together with your fellow pastors to coordinate resources. One goal would be to create a web of support services, academic and social, that would meet the needs of children and families. The adage "united we stand, divided we fall," has never been more true.

Some of you have opened schools. Work with fellow pastors and show them how to do the same. We must work collectively to create alternatives to the public school system. Public officials realize that poor and Black children have little to no choice but to attend neighborhood schools. We must respond by providing needed alternatives. This may mean that we revisit the voucher debate or other public funding sources to support institutions such as yours to do what the public systems have failed to do.

While we strive to establish schools and programs to begin to address the educational needs of our children and communities, we must simultaneously work to transform the public school system. Too many of our children and families depend on public education to totally abandon it. Therefore, we must aggressively work from within to empower the stakeholders: children and parents.

What can be done now? We must get parents into the schools. Challenge your congregations to make their presence felt in their child's failing schools. We share the blame. Our virtual absence from schoolhouses has contributed to their failure. We must return to schools, roll up our sleeves and get to work. This may mean patrolling halls and helping with discipline. This may mean working with untrained teachers and administrators to improve them. This may mean removing incompetent teachers and administrators from our schools. It is true that teachers cannot teach if children are not disciplined. Conversely, children cannot learn in schools if teachers are not disciplined and trained adequately.

In addition, parents must be counseled to take off the veils of denial when it comes to their children's behaviors, abilities and efforts. We must teach parents how to raise children. We must teach them how to work closely with their children and teachers. We must teach them how to support learning from the home. We must teach separated parents to work together to support their children. Parents need support and guidance.

Consider the following actions:

- Create learning centers in your churches. Provide counseling and training for parents.
- Organize meetings with your fellow pastors to share best practices.
- Use your property to house schools and programs that model effective teaching and learning.
- Share your human and physical resources with other churches and community organizations.
- Call upon your congregants to assist you in the design of quality learning-based programs.
- Use churches as information and network centers.
- Use the power of the pulpit to protect our children from others and at times from themselves.
- Visit the schools where the children of your congregants attend. Make your presence felt.
- Invite local principals and teachers to your churches for special Sunday services.
- Target some of your sermons to education. It is sinful not to teach our children. Children who get caught in the prison trap are often illiterate and have dropped out or were pushed out of school.

The Reverend Dr. Martin Luther King Jr. posed this question in the title of one of his books, "Where Do We Go from Here: Chaos or Community?" I ask you to join me and others to step up our efforts to save and educate our children and families. Let us choose community over chaos.

I pray that you receive this letter in the spirit in which it was written.

Book IV

The only thing that interferes with my learning is my education.

—Albert Einstein

Reflections

HELLO, my name is Bernard. I am an addict. I am addicted to stupidity. I continue to believe in a system that does not believe in me. Thank you for listening.

Pupil of the Year: A Personal Reflection - 1977

In *Reflections of an Urban High School Principal*, I told the story of when I received the student of the year award. I found the essay that was written by one of my teachers, Mrs. Shaharagad J. Kleindienst, on behalf of the school. I believe this letter is probably one of the more authentic documents that capture a slice of my youth. What is interesting to me is how what is described in the letter vis-à-vis my character pretty much describes my current character. For those who know me, you be the judge.

Sterling High School
410 Claremont Avenue
Brooklyn, NY 11238
857-4646

PUPIL OF THE YEAR—Re: Bernard Gassaway, DOB: 7/24/60

Bernard completes all his assignments on time or ahead of time without subsequent reminders. Frequently, he voluntarily helps other students catch up when, due to being absent, they are behind, or if they need help in understanding the assignment.

When he encounters difficulty in any area, he now meets the obstacles with calmness and utilizes the reasoning process. Most significantly, he stays with the task until he is successful. His "stick to it" attitude prevails in all his undertakings from sports to academics.

Continuously, he delights us with his search for knowledge and answers to questions. In the English class, it is rare that he is not researching or checking a dictionary to improve his vocabulary—all self-motivated.

Equally as remarkable is the progress Bernard has made in his social life as well as his academic life. He has progressed from a disinterested, sulking, hostile, aggressive marginally productive academic student to one who is now well-liked by his peers and admired by the staff of his school for the positive attitude and leadership he has shown in the last year and a half. Bernard has, additionally, become aware of the need for self-evaluation and setting goals academic and personal. These responsibilities of self-direction he has handled in an extraordinary way.

The most concrete evidence of his responsible behavior is evidenced in his academic excellence and his happiness in family living. For nearly two years, he has maintained a 90+ average in all subjects! Another example of his "togetherness" is his record of attendance and punctuality. He has had nearly perfect attendance and punctuality for nearly two years.

The services Bernard has rendered to his home, school and community are numerous and meritorious.

In the home, his new self-confidence and academic success has brought about positive changes that has brought him closer to his family, and the family members closer to each other. His mother commented recently that when he was a "child of the streets," he was seldom home, fought with his siblings and, in general, appeared disinterested in the family. Now, for nearly two years, he has kept a job, comes home at a decent hour and is interested in the events in the lives of his brothers and sisters and helps them whenever necessary.

Our school also has benefited from his talents and time. Bernard is a very good basketball player and is a member of the school team. This represents a sacrifice on his part, as he holds a part-time job in addition to carrying a heavy study load necessary to ensure the academic excellence he has attempted. Several assembly programs have been made more successful because of his participation reciting poetry, as a quiz program contestant, and for helping other students learn their part. In our Guidance office, he has unselfishly given his time helping to file and mail clerical forms. Frequently, he is called upon to take visitors to our school on a tour of our building. He does a creditable job! As his presentation is not "canned," he bears the responsibility for conveying accurately what is happening at Sterling High School, and what we are trying to accomplish. His presentations have provided an excellent overview of our school's curriculum and objectives from a student's point of view.

Visitors have commented upon how he has "filled them in," and also how polite and enthusiastic he is while conducting the tour.

The community in which Bernard lives also benefited. Recently, out of concern for others, after all of the heavy snowfalls, he shoveled out the walks of almost all of his neighbors, without accepting anything in return. On several occasions, he assisted a handicapped neighbor who was having trouble negotiating the icy streets and saw to it that he safely got to his destination.

Everything already cited demonstrates his positive attitude toward his schoolwork and reflects his self-motivation. I was interested in what caused the dramatic change in Bernard's functioning and what did he see as the motivation for his desire to succeed. This is the answer he gave in response to my question, "What made you make such an enormous change in your life?"

"Hanging out all hours of the night, getting into trouble, was hurting my mother, my grandmother, my family and me. I took the help that was offered to me to get myself together. I realized that if I did not take it and stayed on the streets, jail or getting killed would be my future instead of getting to college. So, I made the move."

Yes, he made the move and we, his teachers, are moved by the efforts and the progress he has made despite numerous obstacles in his life.

Try to be a rainbow in someone's cloud.

—*Maya Angelou*

Mentor Me

Nearly 10 years ago, I attended a community event organized by young folks from southeast Queens. What I experienced continues to this day to rock my faith and challenge my resolve and hope. Here is how I recorded the event.

Wow! I attended a youth rally on Sunday evening. Several hundred youths gathered to participate in what is called "I Love My Life Campaign." The purpose of the campaign is to motivate young people to take control of their lives and stem the tide of senseless violence and killings that plague our communities. This campaign is the brainchild of Erica Ford, Director of Life Camp, Inc. I attended the rally to listen to our youth not as the sage, but as the student.

The rally was led by the youths. I was inspired by their leadership and wisdom. They spoke directly to their peers about their collective responsibility to help each other survive and be positive forces in their community. At one point in the rally, youths who were attending this rally for the first time were asked to introduce their "crew." One particular crew whose members were younger than 12 years old caught my heart and soul, the SSN crew. One member of the group was asked to define SSN. He said, "South Side" then hesitated. Another member proudly stood up and said, "We are SSN, South Side Niggers." I said to myself, "Oh my God! We are in deep trouble." I found it difficult to shake the description that flowed so effortlessly out of the mouth of this child. Moments after the remarks, I approached the SSN. I asked them how they got their name. One boy said, "We were walking down Hillside Avenue and came up with the name." Another boy said, "I wanted to call us South Side Goons." At this point, I asked, "Have you thought about calling yourself SSK?" One boy responded, "South Side Killers." I said, "No! South Side Kings." His puzzled facial expression told the entire story.

I realize more than ever that nothing short of men and women being directly involved in the lives of children will make a bit of difference. They want and need two things: experiences and relationships. Experiences and relationships are what change lives for better or worse. They sustain life and give it meaning and purpose. If our children have limited experiences and relationships, they will have limited lives.

Members of SSN looked at me with a yearning as if to say, "We are all we got. These are my niggers, my friends, my boys, my people. Nobody else is there for us."

Though painful to acknowledge, we should not deny that SSN epitomized a large segment of our community of children. They speak their truth. Who are we to question their reality, especially as "outsiders"?

I do not have the answers. I pray to God every day to deliver a sign. The "I Love My Life Campaign" rally was a sign.

Leadership: A Look Back

I must confess. There were times when I wanted to be the sage. Leadership can become intoxicating. You want to have the answers. You are the center of attention. While you are intoxicated, everything seems fine. I used to experience withdrawal, a sensation that some may describe as an anxiety attack. After working 80- to 100-hour weeks, when the time came for a vacation, I did not know what to do with myself. How do you slow down after going 100 miles an hour?

As a leader, I have experienced many of what Joseph L. Badaracco, Jr. describes as defining moments. The examples that I share will span from my time as a principal to my tenure as a superintendent.

Background

On Friday, April 25, 1997, a windy and rainy day, I began my tenure as principal of Beach Channel High School. It did not take long for me to realize that children were not the top priority for this school community. The school atmosphere was toxic. It appeared as if the teachers conceded the corridors to the students. Fights were frequent. Chaos reigned. Children were aimless. Some adults were apathetic. This was fertile ground for unethical behavior. As I attempted to improve school conditions, I faced a tremendous amount of opposition, mainly from those who benefited from the chaos, confusion, and corruption.

As I tackled issue after issue, the number of anonymous allegations filed against me increased. They ranged from mismanagement to misappropriation of funds. Although I was certain of my innocence, the stress I experienced was overwhelming. I would often struggle to understand why I was facing so much resistance and lack of support simply because of my singular purpose to serve children justly.

Moral Judge and Jury

I consider myself to be the ultimate child advocate. However, I find it ethically challenging when I have to discipline students. Regardless of what happen, I feel like I am punishing the victim. This becomes particularly clear when I meet the parents of children. I recall one day when a female student cursed me out. She called me nearly every profane word imaginable. I contacted her mother and told her she needed to come to the school. When she arrived, she said, "What is the problem? I have to go home and get my dick." I said, "Excuse me." She said, "You heard me!" She then repeated her comment. I immediately thanked her for coming and told her she could leave. I thought, "How could I punish her daughter when she was only doing as she had been taught or had witnessed." Rather than punish the daughter, I sent her to a guidance counselor. I will never forget that day. Though I disciplined many students after this incident, it changed my way of thinking and feeling. I continued to struggle with the challenge of how to redress a wrong knowing that all parties were, in essence, victims. I adopted a philosophy I called "discipline with love." I was thoughtful and deliberate. I was often reminded of when my mother would beat me with a belt or an extension cord. It appeared to hurt her more than it hurt me. It was only when I became a principal that I understood how she felt.

Silence is Betrayal

One of my most significant ethical challenges was to decide whether to continue to work in the New York City Department of Education (DOE). I was totally conflicted. My values and beliefs were in conflict with the leadership of Mayor Bloomberg and Chancellor Klein. It became harder each day to go to work. I felt as if I was swimming upstream while weighted down with ethical burdens. As I visited schools and programs, I would witness the harmful effects of DOE policies. One example was the mayor's program, "New Beginnings," which purported to serve over-age and under-credited students. He and the chancellor spoke glowingly about the benefits of the program. In reality, the children were removed from their schools and placed in what may best be described as dumps. Morally, I could not reconcile the discrepancies between the rhetoric of the city's leadership and their practices. I had to decide: Was it more important to be a team player or a child advocate? I realized that I could not be both. In my book, *Reflections of an Urban High School Principal*, I explained that I could not serve two masters. "You cannot serve children and remain silent while they are being hurt under your watch." I often thought of the words of the poet Durante degli Alighieri, "The hottest places in hell are reserved for those who in times of great moral crisis maintain their neutrality." What I witnessed children go through in some of these dysfunctional programs inspired moral crises. After visiting a plethora of these programs, including prisons and juvenile detention facilities, I could not remain silent. Though I resigned as superintendent on June 30, 2005, I vowed to continue to serve and fight for children from outside of the system. I continue to believe that silence is betrayal.

It is the mind that makes the body.

—*Sojourner Truth*

Do Fathers Matter: My Father

How do I miss what I have never had? Very early, I learned to cope with the reality of not having my father in my life. It became second nature, so I thought.

Every time I go to a new doctor, during the initial visit, I am asked a question about my parents' medical history. When I get to the section about my father's medical history, I answer NA (Not Applicable) or DK (Don't Know). It wasn't until I had my first prostate examination that an awareness of my father's medical history became significant to me. Up to that point, I told myself that my medical history began with me. I now know I was wrong.

Now, my curiosity goes beyond his medical history.

I wonder what my father smelled like. Was his skin rough or smooth? What color were his eyes? Was he bald? Was he tall or short?

Was he a smart child? Did he graduate from high school? Did he go to college or join the military? What did he want to be when he grew up? Did he play sports? Did he have a sense of humor? What jobs did he hold? Was he courageous?

Did he ever hold me lovingly in his arms? Was he proud of me? Did he ever change my diapers? Did he ever push me in a stroller? Did he think about me? Did he have other children? If so, was he a good father to them? Did he have other sons? Did he feel guilty about not being in my life?

How did he feel about my mother? Was she just another woman in his life or was she special? Did he love her? When he first heard that she was pregnant with me, was he happy or upset? Did he suggest she abort me?

Did he have brothers and sisters? Did he know his father? Was his father or father's father a slave? When did the first of my patriarchal lineage arrive as captives on this shore? I wonder about my father's mother and her mother.

Were they raped by their captors? What village and country in Africa did their family come from?

I wonder about my father's cause of death and how old he was when he died. Would knowing this information possibly extend my life or the life of my child?

I remember when my aunt called me one morning after midnight about 25 years ago. She lived on the West Coast. She said, "Bernard, your father died today." I said, "Thank you," and hung up the phone. The next morning, I do not recall even thinking about it. In death as in life, he was irrelevant and barely a thought.

Several years ago, I spoke to my daughter about all of my questions. I asked her if she ever asked herself about my father, her grandfather. She said, "Yes." When she suggested that I try to get the answers to some of my questions, I said, "I am not sure I want to know." She said, "I do not understand. That's confusing." I said, "That is exactly right. I am confused." It took me all of 40-plus years to ask myself the questions. I am not sure how long it will take me to be prepared to hear the answers.

Action Plan for School Personnel: School Revolution, not Reform

"We have locked doors, security officers, metal detectors, surveillance cameras; we follow a daily routine; we have limited bathroom privileges, limited dining options, limited programs, limited rights; we are voiceless; we are trained; we are tracked; we are profiled; we wear uniforms; we are classified; we are segregated according to classification; we carry I.D. cards; we are identified by number; we have gangs; we experience violence; we are assaulted; we are harassed; we are used for research studies; we are used to supporting large industries. Where are we—*school* or *prison*?"

A history of school reforms in America has brought us to the point where there is little difference between schools and prisons both in conditions and operations. This is especially true of school systems that serve Black and poor children. Therefore, the only solution to our educational crisis is a revolution, not reform.

A revolution is necessary because:

- The history of public schools in America is rooted in classism, racism and sexism. Children of the rich and privileged have always received a different education. Nothing has changed over some 400 years in America. The rich, White and privileged receive one form of education, while the Black and poor receive another.
- Public school systems fail because their design is fundamentally and morally flawed. It is unconscionable to have twenty to forty children in a class. It is unconscionable to teach children that they

are inferior. This is achieved not only by what is taught but also by what is not taught.
- Public school children often receive an inferior education, particularly if they are Black or poor. One's education cannot be fulfilled if it does not include knowledge of self. Black people are all but ignored in literature and history courses that are taught in public schools—but for the month of February. Even when Black people are mentioned or shown, they are often depicted as inferior beings. This is as true today as it was pre-Emancipation Proclamation. Any system that fails to recognize the richness of the people it teaches is designed to perpetuate deprivation and dependency.
- Public school systems are more about control and propaganda than about freedom and equality.
- Analyze any public school curriculum and you will find sanitized versions of American history. The truth, harsh as it may be, has become irrelevant in public schools. This is largely driven by ignorance, politics and testing.

A revolution is necessary because an educational system rooted in imperialism and oppression will never educate the oppressed to be free. That would be antithetical to its design. What I propose would require an exodus from what we now know as the public school system. I realize that my recommendations will be difficult to implement and to accept, especially by those oppressed people who believe they have benefited greatly from the very system I wish to abolish.

"Highly educated Negroes denounce persons who advocate for the Negro a sort of education different in some respects from that now given the white man." Carter G. Woodson (The Mis-Education of the Negro, 1933)

Revolutionary New School Design

Design learning environments as villages, not cities. Each adult must care about and know every child. Once the number of children exceeds the capacity of the adults to know them by name and circumstance, the school has exceeded its capacity. No new schools should be built to serve more than 400. I have come to this number based on my nearly 50 years of involvement in public education as a student, teacher and administrator. Furthermore, no school built in the 21st century should resemble schools built in the 19th century. The same can be said for some teaching methodologies (e.g., "talk and chalk.")

Design learning environments to:

- Revive the art of thinking. Our children must exercise thinking just as they exercise their bodies. If the "thinking muscle" is not exercised, it will atrophy.
- Emphasize what children can do rather than what they cannot do.
- Ensure children have freedom over confinement. The current paradigm must shift from teacher-dominated to child-centered.
- Eliminate standardized tests, frivolous homework, grades, report cards and curriculum. These are barriers to healthy learning experiences. Parents and teachers begin test prep as early as pre-k.
- Promote discovery, creativity, exploration and fun.
- Design learning environments that are dynamic rather than static or predictable. Eliminate fixed schedules.
- Design learning environments that are safe but not restrictive. Children cannot learn if their spirits are held captive by fear, distrust and disrespect. Provide children with space to move about freely.
- Design learning environments where children would be free from classism, racism and sexism.
- Design learning environments where conversation replaces lecture. Children learn best when they are respected as beings rather than as objects to receive irrelevant and erroneous information.

- Design learning environments where adults provide positive reinforcement and healthy relationships.
- Design learning environments where adults are non-judgmental and open-minded about creative learning.
- Design learning environments to accommodate children who learn differently and at different times. These environments would recognize that children have different learning styles and different biological clocks. As an adult I discovered I am a visual, kinesthetic and tactile learner, not auditory. I would have probably been an exceptional learner if I attended school from 3:00 AM to 9:00 AM rather than from 9:00 AM to 3:00 PM.

The only solution to our educational crisis is a revolution, not reform.

Book V

The whole world opened to me when I learned to read.
—*Mary McLeod Bethune*

Compilation of Published Articles

Teachers

NEARLY [40] years ago, while serving an 18-month sentence in a New York State Division for Youth detention facility, I met a teacher who taught math in a way I could understand. Before I met him, I was totally turned off to math. My teachers did not explain it in a way I could understand, so I shut down. Here's what I remember about this teacher. He wore his hair in a ponytail. He wore jeans and a t-shirt. He cared about us. He made us feel special. He took some of us fishing. He was nice. He was cool. He was patient. I never forgot his impact on my learning experience.

Thirty years later in 2004, as Senior Superintendent of Alternative Schools and Programs for the City of New York, I remember visiting a classroom located in a prison-like homeless shelter in the Bronx. As I entered the room, I immediately observed about 18 students, from age 17 to 21, packed in a room that probably legally held five people. These students could be described as people of color, Latino and of African ancestry. The shelter reminded me of a building that might be found in a war zone. It was scary. I thought to myself, "It must be hell living here."

Students appeared to be working on individual assignments. There was something surreal about this experience. I was in a classroom. No, I was in an apartment made to look like a classroom. It had the elements: desks, chairs, students and a teacher. Was she a teacher? When I approached her, I noticed her swollen face. It was too big not to notice. I am sure my facial expression gave away the obvious question, "What the hell happened to your face?" She took the liberty and answered my unspoken question. "I had oral surgery yesterday. I could not take off because my students needed me." I am sure I fought back tears. I was in the midst of human misery. I was also in the presence of an unknown, out of sight, angel. She was a teacher not because she came to work, even in pain. She was a teacher because she cared about her students. Their growth and success mattered to her. She knew that her absence would leave them without instruction and care. She understood her students needed to escape, albeit temporarily, from their constant reminder of their homelessness. I remember thinking, "How can they focus and think about school?" The answer to my unspoken question was the teacher. She found a way out of no way. She gave them hope.

I remember visiting another homeless shelter in Brooklyn. It was a one-classroom site. The teacher and teacher's assistant made a classroom out of little or nothing. There were about five students in the class this day, three females and two males. They had at least two things in common: They were Black and illiterate. They ranged in age from 16 to 21. The teacher divided the students into different groups. Some worked on math and others worked on reading and phonics. The teacher asked one young girl if she would read for my colleague and me. The girl looked at the page on the book and began to cry. It was as if she lost her voice. She wanted so much to read for us. Her brain simply shut down. I thought to myself; it must be difficult for her to come to this country and not know the language. You can imagine how shocked I was when I discovered she was born and raised in Brooklyn. I was shocked even further when she said she had attended a local high school as a freshman.

I will never forget the teacher. She was patient. She was focused on her tasks. She did not let us (the visitors) interfere with her work. She was a parent. She cared about her students. Her mission was to get her students to read and to compute, one letter and one number at a time. She was a teacher who chose to work with a group of forgotten people.

I also remember visiting a community-based organization located somewhere in the South Bronx. After signing in, I was directed to go through the doors and make a left turn. There I found the most dynamic individual, all of 5 feet tall, who weighed probably fewer than 100 pounds. She was full of energy and love. She had about 25 adult students crammed into a space that would comfortably fit 15. As was my custom, I introduced myself and asked the students to introduce themselves. They said their names and where they were from. Hello, my name is _____. I am from Dominican Republic, Mexico, Puerto Rico, Ghana, Ivory Coast, Guinea, Mali, and Haiti. I felt so proud of them. Many of the adult students worked at night and came to school in the morning. Some drove taxicabs and some worked in restaurants washing dishes. Some were on welfare. The teacher could not stop praising their efforts. Many of the students simply wanted to learn to read to help their children with homework. One pregnant mother brought me to tears when she said she wanted to learn to read to be able to read street signs and find her way home.

This teacher has never been absent from work in more than 16 years. She probably never had a lunch hour. She takes money out of her pocket and provides her adult students with car fare. I have seen her give food to students to take home. She is a beautiful person. She loves her students. The system only recognizes her as a number. To the families in the South Bronx and to me, she is a beloved teacher. She is a great woman who may never be recognized beyond the walls of her makeshift classroom. For her, that is enough. All she wants is to be able to educate her forgotten students.

As a New York City educator for 18 years, I have been in the presence of greatness. Many teachers are worth their weight in gold. I have seen teachers perform what many may describe as miracles. A teacher touches individual students. A teacher teaches individuals, not classes. A teacher sees the possibilities in her students. A teacher gives hope. A teacher gives voice. A teacher navigates. A teacher explores. A teacher is patient. A teacher learns with his or her students. A teacher discovers. A teacher is a parent. A teacher accepts children as they are, not as he or she would like them to be.

It is a miracle that curiosity survives formal education.

—Albert Einstein

BLAME GAME: A GAME WITHOUT WINNERS

For sure, the one thing most people in the United States of America can agree on is that we are currently faced with an educational crisis. Our children are being outperformed by countries with fewer resources. Children are dropping out of school in record numbers. While schools are failing children across this country, prisons are swelling. So, who is really to blame for our current conditions?

Blame children. "Children fail in school because they do not care! They do not value education. They do not respect authority. They do not respect their parents. They do not know God."

Blame parents. "They do not have control over their children. They expect schools to raise them. They do not even join the PTA."

Blame teachers. "They are responsible for teaching our children. When children fail, teachers fail to teach. They only care about their next pay raise and having summers off."

Blame principals. "Principals are not doing their job. Schools are out of control and children are not learning. They are afraid of the teacher's union."

Blame politicians. "They do not care about children because children do not vote. Politicians are crooks."

Blame universities and colleges. "They fail to train teachers adequately. They are not held accountable to schools, students and families. They analyze the problems and write reports. They do very little to solve problems."

Blame the clergy. "Where are the churches? God needs to be in these schools. Churches can do more."

Blame the system. "The system is corrupt and broken."

Blame money. "If we spent more money on education, children would receive a better education."

Blame racism. "Jim Crow is alive and well in our schools. Black and Latino students are taught to be subservient by a Eurocentric curriculum. That's why there is an achievement gap between Whites and Blacks."

Blame sexism. "Girls are not expected to do well in the sciences and mathematics."

Blame drugs. "Children born of addition cannot learn. They cannot sit still in class. They have Attention Deficit Disorder."

Blame poverty. "Poor children receive a poor education."

This is the final round of the blame game. Remember, the only rule in the blame game is to blame something or someone other than yourself.

Parents blame teachers. Teachers blame parents and children. Principals blame parents, teachers and children. Superintendents blame principals, teachers, parents and children. Politicians blame superintendents, principals, parents, and children. Clergy blame politicians, superintendents, principals, teachers, parents, and children. Everyone blames children. Children blame no one.

The blame game is not fun. I do not want to play anymore.

Suicide by Educator

Suicide by educator is a slow, gradual process. It may lead to an emotional, spiritual or physical death. Children who seek suicide by educator may eventually drop out, go to prison or be killed.

At one time or another, teachers may ask themselves, "Why do so many children commit educational suicide? They do not care about school. They come to class without books or homework. They fail classes and tests. So, why do they come to school?"

"Things never stop. I'm always fighting. I'm tired of having to watch my back. I'm for real. It's crazy. I'm stressed at home and at school. So much is going on in my life. Do you feel me? I don't like school. I can't get a job. I got to get mine. Nobody cares about me. Kids always trying to violate. Damn! I'm tired. It's always something. Stop stressing me. I want out. I want out of my house. I want out of my neighborhood. I want out of school. I want out of …"

School

Children who seek suicide by educator deliberately act in a disruptive manner toward teachers or children, provoking confrontations, failing grades, suspensions, expulsions or arrests. They feel disconnected, uncared for, stressed, confused and angry. They are almost always victims of abuse or neglect. They are deficient in math and reading. To them, school is irrelevant; failure is common; life is rough; fights are frequent. They lash out at school officials both verbally and physically. Anything or anyone may become the target of their anger.

School personnel are not trained to deal with the level of anger they are experiencing with children; as a result, they often respond to them with punishment, suspension, failure or arrest. They say, "He is out of control. Suspend him! Fail him! Arrest him!" Rarely do public and school officials, particularly in urban, poor school districts, address the conditions that caused the children's disruptive behaviors. In most cases, school officials contact the parent(s). Ironically, in a cruel twist of fate, the home is likely a contributor to the source of the child's problems. So, like in school, the child goes home to get punished, even physically beaten. After the child returns to school beaten or suspended, nothing has changed and the behavior is often repeated. This cruel process perpetuates the cycle of stress, confusion and anger.

In urban school settings, administrators respond to student anger with punishment therapy. In New York City schools, for example, a child is more likely to be suspended or arrested for an emotional outburst than to receive counseling. This is especially true since the Division of School Safety merged with the New York City Police Department several years ago. School safety agents have been given increased authority to make arrests. In the name of zero tolerance and because they lack other sound options, school administrators are quick to support student arrests. I am convinced that student arrests have increased exponentially since the merger. The charge of choice is "discon," which is short for disorderly conduct. Any angry child may be subjected to arrest on any given day. They are easy prey for people who look to exercise police powers over powerless people—our children.

In a perverse way, children who seek suicide by educator find comfort in chaos. They curse at adults to get an immediate reaction. They disrupt classes and school to get attention. They gain status and notoriety among their peers by breaking rules. When they are confronted about their behavior, they are adept at shifting the blame. "You don't like me. You're always picking on me." They frequently express what someone has done to them. They usually see themselves as victims, never victimizers. They learn this behavior by watching people in their homes and communities.

Culture of Failure

For children who seek suicide by educator, failure has become synonymous with school. They may have experienced institutional failure from as early as preschool. I believe some children have become immune to it. In fact, failure for many is an anticipated result. They say, "I know I am going to fail." When asked how they know this, they respond, "I just know." It is not uncommon to hear students say, "I *only* failed four classes." Failure has become so common in schools that children who fail all classes may go virtually unnoticed. Parents seem surprised that they were not notified by teachers. Teachers seem surprised that parents were not monitoring their children. This pattern is repeated each marking period. Meanwhile, the children have convinced themselves that school is to failure what crime is to prison.

It is also not uncommon for these children to be sentenced to failure by their parents. I've heard mothers say to their sons, "You are just like your father. You ain't going to amount to nothing just like him." These prophetic words provide a confused child with a psychological blueprint for aberrant behavior.

Some children who seek suicide by educator are in a constant state of denial. They seem surprised or angry when they receive a report card with all failing grades. They ask the teacher, "Why did you fail me?" The typical response to such a question is, "You failed the tests and did not do homework." The teacher fails to see the broader meaning of the student's question. The student knows she did not complete assignments and did poorly on tests. In her mind, she made an effort to come to school, and that should count for something. As a response to the documented failure, the child uses this as an opportunity to engage the teacher in a confrontation. Some teachers unwittingly comply, while others wait until the last minute to tell students their final grades in order to avoid a confrontation. Either scenario results in lose-lose situations for students and teachers.

There are no simple solutions. What can we do?

1. Coordinate social services to support the entire family. We will continue to leave children behind as long as we leave families behind. Poor parenting is a social disease. It, like alcoholism and drug addiction, must be treated. Poor parenting is a plague that

is responsible for the slow death of millions of children. If we were to teach and enrich parents successfully, we would eliminate thousands of corporations that profit directly from familial dysfunction, delinquency, dependency, deprivation and depression, all of which lead to other social maladies.

2. Remove failure from the equation. Failure is what feeds the need for suicide. For a young person who is starved for attention, failure fits the bill. If we feed children failure, that's what they will crave. If a child fails to complete a class sequence satisfactorily, why do we require him to repeat the entire sequence? Why do we excessively test children in the name of accountability? Clearly, we need to rethink our methods of assessment and instruction.

3. Replace failure with praise. Seek every opportunity to praise these children. They are often deprived of what so many take for granted—kindness and praise. Schools and community organizations should incorporate kindness into their culture. Good morning. Hello. You look nice today. You have a nice smile. Thank you. All of these niceties take little effort but have tremendous value.

4. Support teachers. Fight to defeat the external forces that prevent good, creative teachers from teaching children. Like parents and students, good teachers lose hope. They too are often beaten down by the system.

5. Protect children. They need positive reinforcement. They need comfort, care and attention—not punishment.

6. Provide children and parents with options. The current school paradigms, public and private, are not sufficient. We need to do more than think outside of the box; we need to come up with other shapes and designs.

Children who seek suicide by educator are victims of their environments. They have been dealt an unfair hand in life. We, society in general, have failed these children. Because we have not figured out how to "fix" them, we beat them. We punish them. We label them. We kill them. Listen carefully when a child says, "Nobody cares about me. So why should I care?"

THE NEW YORK CITY SCHOOL SYSTEM IS NOT BROKEN

I have spent a large part of this past year trying to figure out how to improve the New York City Public School System from the outside. I have come to the following conclusion: The New York City School System is not broken. It is doing what it was designed to do.

People often query, "Why can't the New York City government get the schools to work? After all, they spend nearly 15 billion dollars annually [23 in 2015]." To them I say, again, "The system does work. It was designed to promote uniformity and conformity among its participants, thus, the standards movement. In large urban areas, schools in effect are used to warehouse, not educate, a large number of children (currently, New York City public school enrollment is slightly over 1 million children). Overcrowding, underachievement, high dropout rates and crime are all expected outcomes of warehousing.

Here's what we know. One man's failure may be another man's reward.

We know numerous upstate communities are highly dependent on New York City's residents to fill their prisons. Approximately 66% of the upstate prisoners come from New York City. We know that at least 50% of all New York State detainees do not have high school diplomas. We know that these individuals come from poor neighborhoods that have a disproportionate number of failing schools. We know that at least 50% of all state detainees are African-American, though they only account for 16% of the state's population. Latinos make up 28% of the state's prisoners while only representing 15% of the state's population [The Correctional Association of New York]. We also know conservatively that 50% of African-American males are either dropped or pushed out of New York City public schools (the figure is probably higher when you factor in students who never make it out of junior or middle school).

We know prisons are proportionately built at a higher rate than schools. Since the early 1980s, an additional 36 prisons have been built in New York State. Currently, there are 80 state prisons (including juvenile detention). From a personnel standpoint, there is a correction officer to inmate ratio of 1:3 in the state prisons [Some of NYS prison have begun to close].

We know there is a correlation between the prison population and education failure. When children are not educated, demand is generated for more prisons. Why do you think there was so much opposition from upstate republicans to give New York City additional money for schools? If schools were to educate New York City children successfully, rural upstate communities would suffer because many are dependent on city residents to fill their prisons.

We know upstate politicians fought hard to prevent the city from getting additional school funding. They need not worry. Additional funding for New York City schools may not translate into an improved school system. As long as the system remains the same, you can spend 28 billion dollars and little will change for the majority of the children. School and government officials will find a way to divert the money. Look at how the Department of Education is currently wasting millions of dollars.

We know they are spending hundreds of millions of dollars to hire consultants to fix the system. The largest provider of professional development services for New York City teachers is an Australian-based company. Although school principals will never admit it publicly, many are forced to purchase professional development services from this company. They have no choice.

We know the people who are impacted the most by the New York City education system have virtually no say in its design. Europeans are currently performing the redesign.

As I previously stated, the system is not broken. It is doing what it was designed to do.

African-American scholars have long fought to influence the New York City curriculum. There is a legitimate claim that the children who make up the largest part of the system cannot find any significant evidence of their people's history in the school curriculum. Although documents have been prepared to begin to address this gross omission, the Board of Education has rejected them. No surprise. For city officials to correct this travesty of exclusion, they would be required to hire Africans or people of African ancestry to provide professional development services to schools, similar to the Australian deal. It would also require the school system to recognize that Black history began long before Africans arrived on North American shores as victims of chattel slavery. To do it right, it would cost the system billions of dollars to correct all of the misinformation and propaganda. Teachers and administrators must be retrained. New books must be written and purchased. I surmise even if these efforts were successful, it is easier to train the mind than it is to train the heart. At this point, I would welcome an educational system that focuses on truth, relevance and student interests.

As I speak to numerous groups, teachers often ask me, "What can I do to help the children I have pledged to serve?" I say, "Stay true to your principles. Be prepared to make the ultimate sacrifice for our children. If you are a teacher of history, you are culturally and ethically required to teach the truth, although it is your job to teach the lies. As long as children are required to take 'tests,' you are required to prepare them. You need to figure out where you will draw the line. That is an individual decision."

Here are some specific recommendations to confront the educational reality of our children:

- Parents should organize and open learning institutes in their communities. Use the charter school structure.
- Parents should advocate for funding to follow the child—a form of vouchers. This funding should be available to all city residents to support their child's education, regardless of the parents' choice of educational providers, including home education or homeschooling.
- Grassroots community-based organizations should open learning

institutes using the charter school structure or establish independent learning institutes.
- Parents should boycott all standardized testing of their children. The purpose of testing is to fund the testing and publishing industries. A well-trained teacher can provide students with meaningful assessments.
- Establish learning cooperatives. Concentrate brain trusts in specific communities. We know where our human resources are needed. We know where our children are being targeted.
- Home educate your child/children. Revive the right that parents are the first teachers. Work with other like-minded parents to educate your children. There is no natural law that says education is reserved for 8 A.M. to 3 P.M. If you are a parent, you have at least two jobs. One is to earn a living for your family. The second, and more important, is to raise and educate your children. Do not abrogate this important responsibility to an outside entity.
- Design learning institutes that recognize children have different learning styles and different timetables for learning. The current system demands uniformity and conformity. It is designed to teach all children the same information on the same day at the same time. It does not acknowledge that children have different learning styles and different timetables for learning.

Unprotected Children

Today's unprotected children are tomorrow's unprotected adults, unless…

Unprotected children are raised to live in the moment. They do not see a past or future. If there is a tomorrow, it is a nightmare, not a dream. In response to parental and societal neglect and rejection, these children create their own world. They do not respect or value life because no one has taught them respect. They resort to violence as a preacher resorts to prayer. They casually converse among themselves about drugs, sex and money. They feed failure and fill prisons. These children and their children are sentenced to poverty, pain and prison by a generation of adults who selfishly fail to protect them.

As I visit real and virtual prisons, I am compelled to ask, "What will it take to protect our children? What price is too high?"

As our children morph into people we fear and misunderstand, we ask, "What happened to them?" Instead, we should ask, "What have we done to them?"

"I dress to impress. I wear baggy pants and big t-shirts because I want to fit in. If wearing du-rags allows me to blend into my environment, I will wear du-rags. If having a cell phone demonstrates that I am cool, I will carry a cell phone. In fact, I will carry two or three cell phones. If speaking a certain way gets me to blend in, I will speak that way. If having sex makes me popular, I will have sex—yes, even without condoms. If looking hard is good and necessary for survival, I will look hard. If wearing shine brings me attention, I will wear it even if I get jacked for it. If being arrested is a rite of passage, I will get arrested. If failing in school is cool, I will fail. I do not care what you think. I want to be accepted. I want to be known. I want to be respected. Why should I change? It is not about right or wrong. It is about survival. I do what I have to do."

In the absence of adult protection and out of necessity, far too many children have come to rely on the art of camouflage. They learn to blend into their environment as a means of survival. "Because of our [adult] contradictory behavior, children become confused. In order to protect themselves, they turn to people who look like them and speak their language. This protection may come in the form of weapons, gangs, or complete withdrawal from society" (Gassaway, 2006). They may create their own culture and norms. As a result, these children are often misunderstood and even feared by adults.

Some find it easy to lay blame on children for their beliefs and behaviors. We say, "Things were different when we were children. We respected our elders. Schools were good." To this I say, "The grass was never greener. In fact, many of us never had grass." Time has a way of distorting reality. This distortion widens the gulf that exists between children and adults.

Our children are as vulnerable today as we were years ago. I am forty-six years old, and I continue to wear psychological scars that I received when I was a child. It pains me when I see people in authority (this includes parents and school personnel) speaking harsh, piercing, damaging language to children. Children are called stupid, dumb, Special Ed and worse. I recently heard two school officials tell a twelve-year-old child within a five-minute period, "You are irresponsible." Imagine the impact of these words on this child whose only fault may be his inner, unspoken confusion. I have no doubt that this child has been psychologically scarred by the repeated "irresponsible" label. Unprotected and uncorrected, how do you think he will behave in the future?

We have a tendency to think that children today are more prepared to accept the harsh reality of their existence, particularly children who live in neighborhoods that can easily be compared to war zones. This is a huge mistake. Though we all experience violence, children experience it through different lenses. They may experience violence with a greater level of resiliency, not to be confused with immunity. For example, unprotected children who frequently experience local violent episodes, a random fight, shooting, or stabbing, may appear to take it in stride. I would argue their psyche is negatively affected. They are afraid and often do not know where to turn. There are no safe havens for many of our children. As a result, they turn inward and accept violence as a necessary condition of life. They readily accept violence as a required first response to any situation.

I have learned the unprotected child's reality is not unique to American children. Sadly, I find what our children experience in American, to a large degree, is not much different from what children face across the globe: racism, armed conflict, displacement, high-risk sex, voicelessness, incarceration, homelessness, unemployment, illiteracy, abuse, exploitation, destructive media, drugs, guns, hunger, peer pressure, crime, violence and poverty.

Where Do We Go from Here?

No more speeches, panels, covenants, forums or emergency meetings. We must demonstrate responsible behavior. We must protect children with our actions. We must learn to listen to children. How much time on average do you spend with your child daily? Some children may go through childhood never having a conversation with any adult for more than ten minutes. When was the last time you had an eye-to-eye conversation with a child? How long did you listen without offering your "wisdom"?

I know it is not enough to focus only on the child. Programs and policies must focus on the entire family—mother, father, sister and brother. We protect children by keeping families healthy and whole.

Future generations will suffer as does this current generation of children until we deal directly with causes that perpetuate dysfunctional families. Dysfunctional families are malignant social cancers. They exist because families and communities are not empowered or educated to be self-sufficient. Our system teach and support dependency. This is a by-product of a society rooted in racism, sexism and classism. We have had a war on poverty and a war on crime, both of which have been lost. One of the few wars that have been won in this country is the war on families. Someone has figured out that if you disrupt the family order, you destroy the people. This pathology is real. Dysfunctional families create dysfunctional communities, which in turn create dysfunctional societies. This is what we currently have in spite of the superficial rhetoric to the contrary.

Though "real change" may not come in my lifetime, I want my life to be about change. I find it difficult to celebrate in the face of neglect, hunger, poverty and pain. I find it difficult to celebrate when so many children around the world are suffering. There is something morally corrupt about what is happening to our children as many of us sit silently. To paraphrase Martin Luther King Jr., there comes a time when silence is betrayal. That time is now.

On a recent horseback riding trip with my twelve-year-old daughter, Atiya, we came across a family of Canadian geese walking in the middle of the trail, two adults—one male and one female—and five goslings. As the horses came too close for comfort, the adult geese stretched their long black necks and began to make a loud hissing sound, as they placed themselves between the horses and their offspring. It appeared as if they were prepared to protect their young at any cost, including death.

As I think about this experience, I ask myself, "Who is there to protect our children when they are confronted with danger? Who is there to protect our children when they are miseducated? Who is there to protect our children from ill-meaning adults? Who is there to protect our children from themselves?"

I am so fearful for my daughter's generation. If things remain constant, she will grow up in a society not unlike the one her mother and I grew up in. Like the Canadian geese, we must be prepared to protect our children at any cost. What cost are you willing to pay to protect our children?

Action Plan for Policymakers: The Mis-Evaluation of Governor Andrew Cuomo

Over the course of his tenure, Governor Cuomo will affect public education in New York State profoundly for over two million children. The significance of his influence has not been determined. While he is right to be frustrated with over a decade of no significant progress in education, he is wrong to direct his dissatisfaction toward teachers. Cuomo should resist the temptation to focus only on ineffective teachers. Rather, he should focus on how people become teachers and how they are supported. To use a business analogy, one should go to the manufacturer and correct the flaws in the design or, if necessary, change the designer. In this case, Cuomo should focus on the colleges and universities producing teachers and on a state education department that allows alternative routes for entering the teaching field. If Cuomo is serious about improving the quality of education for all children, he should consider the observations of a 25-year educator who has served as teacher, assistant principal, principal, and superintendent in New York City.

First, Cuomo should direct his education advisors to examine teacher preparatory programs. They should identify best practices and require them across all New York public colleges and universities. They should do the same after examining the best induction programs around the world, including the medical profession, the military, and police and fire academies. Our current method of recruiting people to teach is fundamentally flawed, contributing to large numbers of ineffective teachers.

Second, Cuomo's current proposal to hire outside organizations to run so-called failing schools does not seem plausible. It is experimental.

I recommend that Cuomo fully embrace the African "it takes a village to raise a child" framework. Joyce Epstein's (2001, 2010) overlapping spheres of influence, which are rooted in this framework, provide a good place to start. The idea of school, family, and community collaborating to support the whole child is likely the best approach to improving outcomes for children. The outside organization approach, as being proposed, is too risky and may not work—or at least there is no evidence to show it has. Instead, work with schools, families and communities to develop organic and strategic relationships, which can lead to effective collaborations.

Third, Cuomo should focus on the work of central and district offices. How does he hold them accountable as he is holding schools accountable? Closing schools alone will not work. Cuomo and others must figure out ways to hold local educational agencies accountable. It is not enough to blame and to punish victims of a system that failed to support them. Principals and teachers are trying to redress many of the ills of society. To quote a line from Edgar Allan Poe's *The Cask of Amontillado*, "A wrong is unredressed when retribution overtakes its redresser." Do not allow central and district offices to stay out of harm's way while scapegoating teachers and principals for the offices' failure to support them strategically and effectively.

I agree with Cuomo that ineffective teachers must go—immediately! However, a sizeable percentage of their replacements are likely to experience the same fate unless there is an effort to change how people become teachers and how teachers train and develop once on the job. Whom should we blame? Not teachers. They, like the children, are victims of the system. Nevertheless, the harm that ineffective teachers do to children cannot be ignored while we determine solutions to this most profound problem.

I also agree it is imperative that a fair teacher evaluation system be created that accurately measures teacher effectiveness. However, while we may agree that the current system is flawed, it is illogical to replace it with another flawed and unfair system. Before Cuomo uses student standardized test results to evaluate teachers, he must correct the flawed tests. This cannot be ignored!

I told a group of aspiring administrators recently that it is their responsibility to educate their city and state elected officials, who are largely ignorant of what is happening in city and state schools. This is my attempt to inform anyone who will "listen."

In short, I recommend Cuomo take the following actions:

1. Establish a state-of-the-art teacher training and development program. Include colleges and universities in the planning. Focus on how people become teachers. Develop the profession. Create an exemplary teacher induction program—on par with the medical profession.
2. Create a fair teacher evaluation system. Invite the best researchers, scholars, business leaders and education practitioners to a summit and do not leave without a fair evaluation system. Shift from the current political discussion on teacher evaluation to an educational one.
3. Revamp the current testing program because testing has become a large industry driven by greed. Remove the profit incentive from the equation. Focus on ways to improve assessments. Again, gather the best thinkers (from our prestigious colleges and universities along with educational practitioners) to devise an accurate and fair assessment that measures the learning and performance of our children.
4. Focus on reforming failing school systems. Focusing on "failing schools" is blaming the victim and enabling abusers to continue the abuse.
5. Fix the New York State Education Department. Have an independent evaluator advise how to make it relevant and resourceful. Its staffing and organization do not suffice to support districts and schools.
6. Focus attention on New York City's DOE. Uncover fiscal mismanagement. I know that an independent auditor can uncover at least $1 billion in waste.

7. Determine a way to minimize the DOE's constant changes. Each chancellor changes procedures and policies continually, seeding chaos and confusion. This does not help students, parents, principals or community stakeholders who work on improving the school system.

I believe that if Governor Cuomo were to follow the above recommendations, he would significantly affect education for millions of children in New York State. For the sake of our children, I hope he listens and responds.

REFERENCES

Brody, L. (2014, August 14). New York City students show progress on tougher tests. *The Wall Street Journal*.

Bryant, R. (2015, June). Course, counselor, and teacher gaps: Addressing the college readiness challenge in high-poverty high schools. CLASP. Retrieved from http://www.clasp.org/resources-and-publications/publication-1/CollegeReadinessPaperFINALJune.pdf

Clarke, M. (2014, May 19). Prison education programs threatened. *Prison Legal News*. Retrieved from https://www.prisonlegalnews.org/news/2014/may/19/prison-education-programs-threatened/

Campaign for Fiscal Equity v. State of New York State, 86 NY2d 307, 316 [1995] [CFE I].

Campaign for Fiscal Equity, Inc. v. State, 537 744 NYS2d 130 (NYApp.Div.2002)

Coley, R. J. & Barton, P. E. (2006). Lock up and locked out: An educational perspective on the U.S. prison population. *Educational Testing Service*, Policy Information Report.

Davis, L. M., Steele, J. L., Bozick, R., Williams, M. V., Turner, S., Miles, N. V., Saunders, J., & Steinberg, P. S. (2014). How effective is correctional education, and where do we go from here? The results of a comprehensive evaluation. Santa Monica, CA: RAND Corporation, 2014. Retrieved from www.rand.org/content/dam/rand/pubs/research_reports /RR500/RR564/RAND_RR564.pdf

Epstein, J. L. (2001). *School, family, and community partnership: Preparing educators and improving schools*. Boulder, CO: Westview Press.

Epstein, J. L. (2010). *School, family, and community partnership: Preparing *educators and improving schools* (2nd ed.). Boulder, CO: Westview Press.

Every Student Succeeds Act of 2015. (2015). S. 1177.

Ferguson, H. B., Bovaird, S., & Mueller, M. P. (2007, October). The impact of poverty on educational outcomes for children. *Paediatric Child Health. 12*(8), 701-706. Retrieved from http://www.ncbi.nlm.nih.gov/pmc/articles/PMC2528798/

Fessenden, F. (2012, May 11). A portrait of segregation in New York City's schools. *The New York Times*. Retrieved from http://www.nytimes.com/interactive/2012/05/11/nyregion/segregation-in-new-york-city-public-schools.html

Gassaway, B. (2006). *Reflections of an urban high school principal*. Jamaica, NY: XenoGass, ALG.

Gassaway, B. (2006, April 15). Invisible Black boys become invisible Black men unless.... Retrieved from http://www.bernardgassaway.com/InvisibleBlackBoys.pdf

Gassaway, B. (2006, June 1). The New York City school system is not broken. Our Time Press. Retrieved from http://ourtimepress.com/?p=3147

Gassaway, B. (2006, August 10). Parents mind your own business. Retrieved from http://www.bernardgassaway.com/Parents%20Mind%20Your%20Own%20Business.pdf

Gassaway, B. (2006, October 27). School revolution, not reform. The Wave. Retrieved from http://www.rockawave.com/news/2006-10-27/Columnists/080.html

Gassaway, B. (2006, December 1). Unprotected children. Retrieved from http://www.bernardgassaway.com/Unprotected%20Children.pdf

Gassaway, B. (2007, March 15). An open letter to Black clergy. Retrieved from http://www.bernardgassaway.com/An%20Open%20Letter%20to%20Black%20Clergy.pdf

Gassaway, B. (2007, April 13). Suicide by educator. The Wave.

Retrieved from http://www.rockawave.com/news/2007-04-13/Columnists/035.html

Gassaway, B. (2008, February 22). Teachers. Teachers College Record. http://www.tcrecord.org ID Number: 15025.

Gassaway, B. (2008, September 14). The blame game is a game without winners. The Wave. Retrieved from http://www.rockawave.com/news/2007-09-14/Columnists/028.html

Gassaway, B. (2015, March 10). The mis-evaluation of New York governor Andrew Cuomo. Retrieved from http://www.blacknews.com/news/mis-evaluation-public-education-problems-new-york-governor-andrew-cuomo/#.VoKYIml6jvM

Glancy, E., Fulton, M., Anderson, L., Zinth, J. D., Millard, M., & Delander, B. (2014, October). Blueprint for College Readiness (Denver, CO: Education Commission of the States, Retrieved from http://www.ecs.org/docs/BlueprintforCollegeReadiness.pdf.

Gordon, H. R. D., & Weldon, B. (2003). The impact of career and technical education programs on adult offenders: Learning behind bars. *Journal of Correctional Education, 54*(4), 200-209.

Hall, E., & Karanxha, Z. (2012). School today, jail tomorrow: The impact of zero tolerance on the over-representation of minority youth in the juvenile system. PowerPlay: *A Journal of Educational Justice 4*(1), 1-30.

Handberry v. Thompson, No. 96 Civ. 6161 (S.D.N.Y. Nov.20, 1996).

Handberry v. Thompson, 446 F. 3d 335 n.6 (2d Cir. 2006).

Harlow, C. W. (2003). *Education and correctional populations. Bureau of Justice Statistics special report.* Washington, DC: US Department of Justice.

Harris, E. A. (2015, August 4). New York City task force targets cheating by teachers and principals. Retrieved from http://www.nytimes.com/2015/08/05/nyregion/new-york-city-task-force-targets-cheating-by-teachers-and-principals.html?_r=0

Herbert, B. (2007, June 9). *School to prison pipeline. New York Times.*

Retrieved from http://select.nytimes.com/2007/06/09/ opinion/09herbert.html

Ismailova, Z. (2007). *Prison education program participation and recidivism.* M.A. dissertation. Pittsburg, Pennsylvania: Duquesne University. Retrieved from ProQuest Digital Dissertations database.

Kim, C. Y., Losen, D. J., & Hewitt, D. T. (2010). *The school-to-prison pipeline: Structuring legal reform.* New York, NY: New York University Press.

Kucsera, J., & Orfield, G. (2014). *New York State's extreme school segregation: Inequality, inaction and a damaged future.* Los Angeles, CA: UCLA Civil Rights Project.

Lacour, M., & Tissington, L. D. (2011, July). The effects of poverty on academic achievement. *Educational Research and Reviews, 6*(7), 522-527. Retrieved from http://www.academicjournals.org/ERR

Lee, B., Schaefer, S., & Messner-Zindell, S. (2007). School or the streets: Crime and California's dropout crisis. *Fight Crime: Invest in Kids California.*

Nuttall, J., Hollmen, L., & Staley, E. M. (2003). The effect of earning a GED on recidivism rates. *Journal of Correctional Education, 54*(3), 90-94.

LoBuglio, S. (2005). Time to reframe politics and practices in correctional education. *National Center for the Study of Adult Learning and Literacy, 2*(4). Retrieved from http://www.ncsall.net/ index.html@id=560.html

Mitra, D. (2011). *Pennsylvania's best investment: The social and economic benefits of public education.* Retrieved from http://www.elc-pa.org/wp-content/uploads/2011/06/BestInvestment_Full_Report_6.27.11.pdf

OECD (2013), Education at a glance 2013: OECD indicators, OECD Publishing. Retrieved from http://www.oecd.org/edu/eag2013%20%28eng%29--FINAL%2020%20June%202013.pdf

Payne, C. M. (2008). *So much reform, so little change: The persistence of failure in urban schools.* Harvard Education Press.

Reardon, S. F. (2011). The widening academic achievement gap between the rich and the poor: New evidence and possible explanations. In R. Murnane & G. Duncan (Eds.), *Whither Opportunity? Rising Inequality and the Uncertain Life Chances of Low-Income Children.* New York, NY: Russell Sage Foundation Press.

Rothstein, R. (2014, November 12). The racial achievement gap, segregated schools, and segregated neighborhoods—A constitutional insult. Commentary. Washington, DC: The Economic Policy Institute. Retrieved http://www.epi.org/publication/the-racial-achievement-gap-segregated-schools-and-segregated-neighborhoods-a-constitutional-insult/

Rothstein, R., & Santow, M. (2012). A different kind of choice. Working Paper. Washington, DC: The Economic Policy Institute. Retrieved from http://www.epi.org/files/2012/Different_Kind_Of_Choice.pdf

Sarra, D., & Olcott, L. (2007). Day at Osborne school. *Phi Delta Kappan, 89*(1), 68-70.

Schott Foundation (2015). Black lives matter: The Schott 50-state report on public education and Black males. Retrieved from http://www.blackboysreport.org/2015-black-boys-report.pdf

Sharkey, P. (2010). Converging evidence for neighborhood effects on children's test scores: An experimental, quasi-experimental, and observational comparison. Paper prepared for the Brookings Institution Project on Social Inequality and Educational Disadvantage: New Evidence on How Families, Neighborhoods and Labor Markets Affect Educational Opportunities for American Children. Retrieved from http://cas.uchicago.edu/workshops/education/files/2010/03/Burdick-Will-Ed-Workshop-20100301.pdf

Spangenberg, G. (2004). Every nine seconds in America a student becomes a dropout. *Current Issues in Correctional Education.* Council for Advancement of Adult Literacy.

Steurer, S. J., Smith, L. G., & Tracey, A. (2001). Three state recidivism study. *Office of Correctional Education, United States Department of Education,* 1-63.

Sullivan, E. (2007). Deprived of dignity. Degrading treatment and abusive discipline in New York City & Los Angeles public schools. *National Economic and Social Rights Initiative.*

Sum, A., Khatiwada, I., McLaughlin, J., & Palma, S. (2009). The consequences of dropping out of high school: Joblessness and jailing for high school dropouts and the high cost for taxpayers. Center for Labor Market Studies Northeastern University. Boston, Massachusetts. Retrieved from http://www.northeastern.edu/clms/wp-content/uploads/The_Consequences_of_Dropping_Out_of_High_School.pdf

United States Department of Justice, Bureau of Justice Statistics. (2002, June). Recidivism of prisoners released in 1994. Retrieved from http://www.ojp.usdoj.gov/bjs/pub/press/rpr94pr.htm

Vacca, J. S. (2004). Educated prisoners are less likely to return to prison. *Journal of Correctional Education, 55*(4), 297-305.

Vernick, S. H., & Reardon, R. C. (2001). Career development programs in corrections. *Journal of Career Development, 27*(4), 265-277.

Wade, B. (2007). Studies of correctional education programs. *Adult Basic Education and Literacy Journal, 1*(1), 27-31.